THE CLASS OF '71

A TALE OF DESEGREGATION IN GAMECOCK CITY

WARREN MOISE

Dedicated to J. Grady Locklear, the soul of Gamecock City.

For a well-documented look back at the Class of
'71 in its prime, visit Dave Pettigrew's wonderful
website at http://www.edmundshigh.com/

Thanks to Arlene Brown for her expertise and advice.

Special thanks to Kate Jennings Basten for all your help.

Table of Contents

Prologue

The Road to Gamecock City

One hundred or so miles northwest of Charleston, South Carolina is a small town soaked in the smoky brine of Southern history called Sumter, but better known by locals as the "Gamecock City." A few miles away in the county lies Gamecock City's sister municipality, Stateburg, a town promoted and lived in by Revolutionary War General Thomas Sumter and his family. Stateburg's main street was the King's Highway (i.e., South Carolina's main road from Charleston into the central back country). British, Loyalist, and American troops traveled the King's Highway throughout the war.

After the Revolution, Stateburg became a gathering of eagles. Set in what's known as the High Hills of the Santee, Stateburg was covered with a green quilt of pine trees, cotton plantations with beautiful houses, and manicured English gardens. The rich and famous from across the western world lived, visited, and died there. Vice-President Aaron Burr passed through these roads, as did President Martin Van Buren, whose son, Abraham, married Stateburg belle Angelica Singleton Van Buren who essentially became the First Lady. Civil War diarist Mary Boykin Chesnut lived there, and Secretary of War Joel Poinsett died in Gamecock County on a visit.

Sans Souci in the High Hills was the summer home of the Rutledge brothers. Remember the Rutledge Brothers? Edward Rutledge, the middle brother, signed the Declaration of Independence. His younger brother, Hugh, was a Chancellor in Equity (i.e., an equity circuit judge). The eldest brother, John Rutledge was the first Governor of South Carolina, the one who got us through the Revolutionary War. You might even say that for a time during the Revolution, the government of South Carolina was located wherever you found John Rutledge's horse. He later became Chief Justice of the United States Supreme Court before his death on July 23, 1800.

But the brightest stars, socially speaking, in Gamecock County were Thomas Sumter's son, Thomas Sumter Jr. (America's first Ambassador to Brazil), and his daughter-in-law, whose name is so long it could be a sentence: Nathalie Béatrix Marie-Louise Sumter de Lage de Volude.

Nathalie was honest-to-God, *real* royalty, as she was the daughter of a French count and marquise. Her mom was friends with Marie Antoinette and thus linked to the French Court of King Louis XVI, at least until the bottom dropped out of the court at Versailles (a.k.a. the French Revolution) and heads began to roll. In the chaotic aftermath, Nathalie was shipped off to America. Eventually, she was taken into the household of Aaron Burr and married Thomas Sumter Jr. Their son, Thomas De Lage Sumter, became owner of the family plantation and served in Congress for a time. By the time that the War Between the States exploded, Gamecock County was the wealthiest county in South Carolina. French Counsel DeChoseul visited on at least one occasion, and

Italian Count Binda spent so much time in Stateburg that he fell in love with, and wedded, one of the Sumter daughters.

Yeah, so apparently, Gamecock County was the place to be.

Until you take into account that this paradise was a ticking bomb. It was a white aristocratic society resting on unsteady colonnades of seething black slaves. They lived and died in the furnace-like heat of their squalid slave cabins. But one day the legacies of those white and black slaveowners and the resentment of their angry black slaves would be laid on the front doorstep of none other than – you guessed it – the Class of 1971.

• • •

It was a warm morning in 1970. I walked barefoot onto the front porch to retrieve the mail. Amongst the letters was a cheaply designed mimeographed flyer from the Gamecock City School Board of Trustees entitled "Report to Parents." The generic look of it made me think it was likely sent to every student in District 17. I padded to the front steps, sat down, and read it. The Report to Parents confirmed that the whole Potemkin Village of "separate-but-equal" was about to come crashing down on our heads like a rotted roof. Of course, that's not exactly what the letter said, and frankly, I don't remember the exact words, but that's what that letter *meant*.

Now, see, that rotted roof wouldn't crash down on the heads of the people who cre*ated* this "separate-but-equal" crap, mind you, but on the heads of young boys and girls who had nothing to do with it. After all, these rising high school seniors couldn't even legally buy Boone's Farm Apple Wine yet, let alone *vote*.

When the Class of '71 matriculated into First Grade, three discrete school systems existed side-by-side in Gamecock County: one was white, the other was black, and the third was comprised of Native Americans. Twelve years later, when the Class of '71 graduated high school, there was just one school system, one comprised of all races in the county. This is the story of how the heck we got there.

CHAPTER ONE

The Law of Unintended Consequences

I began my academic career in 1959 in the classroom of Miss Edna Boney at Central Elementary School. We had no air conditioning at Central, so we sweated like pigs through our clothes all day. In fact, until roughly the mid-1960s, students in Gamecock City attended school in facilities not far removed from the era when dinosaurs walked the earth. The playgrounds were just big areas of grassless, honest southern dirt. At Central, there was no playground equipment, except big red rubber balls, suitable for playing head ball, a game that's similar to tennis, but with no net and where your head is the racket. The boys tended to play marbles. Of course, there were always football or baseball games if a student brought a football, or a baseball and bat.

Central School consisted of three massive buildings, two of which had huge white columns and the third of which had smaller columns and a huge cupola. These beautiful structures (all of which are now destroyed) were probably as large as the capitol buildings of some states, or even countries.

My peers at Central Elementary were all white, except for a smattering of Asian kids. Black students? They weren't allowed into the white schools, and, theoretically, vice versa. An all-black school was a block away from Central. A large two-story building with a gymnasium, cafeteria, library, and band room, it was called Lincoln High School.

For a brief period in the mid-1960s, the black and white schools had a "freedom-of-choice" arrangement. Under this deal, the black and white schools largely remained segregated. You might say that it was voluntary segregation. If a black student chose to attend a white school and get his behind kicked by the class bullies on a regular basis, well, he had that freedom. On the other hand, if a white student were to choose a black school and get harassed every day, that was OK, too. Few to no white students were breaking down the doors to get into black schools, but on paper, it presented a colorable claim of equality.

This "freedom-of-choice" scheme continued until our senior year, when the powers-that-be threw in the towel and every school in town was completely desegregated.

Despite ugly Movietone Newsreels to the contrary, many students in the Class of '71 anticipated that total desegregation was going to be a good thing. The prevailing mindset among white kids seemed to be that: "Hey, we're going to have to live and work together the rest of our lives, so we might as well go to school together." It was peace and love, dude.

Maybe this "prevailing mindset" was all in my head, because another philosophy held by radicals on the far left and far right seemed to be that a race war might not be a bad thing.

There were legal problems to this sudden and massive desegregation, of course, the greatest of which was the Law of Unintended Consequences. Like Murphy's Law, the Law of Unintended Consequences wasn't enacted by Congress, but it went something like this: the Justice Department and the

Supreme Court thought that when black students and white students were compelled to give up their old alma maters and come together, it was going to be all flowers everywhere.

As it turned out, many Lincoln High students didn't want any flowers that grew at Edmunds High. They just wanted their old school back. They wanted their boo-dog mascot back. They wanted their traditions back. The former Lincoln students wanted their marching band, school colors, and yearbook back. They were very clear with the Gamecock City School Board of Trustees about these things. White students didn't want to have their traditions thrown upside down either.

This mass rejection of complete desegregation wasn't limited to Gamecock City. Blacks in St. Louis, Missouri, felt the same way, as did those in Topeka, Kansas, and other towns across the South. Many black parents didn't want their children attending white schools. In South Carolina's upstate, the old Seneca High School, a white school scheduled to reopen as an integrated elementary school, was burned in August of 1970, and local officials suspected arson. Black parents boycotted classes in the Easley and Grays schools in South Carolina's upstate. Black parents also protested the closure of what were formerly all-black schools in Robertsville and Simpsonville, South Carolina.

The racial tension surrounding complete desegregation transcended all boundaries. Mexican Americans in Houston, Texas threatened a boycott, unless they could be designated in a separate racial classification from whites. They argued that integration harmed them academically. A black man in Miami shot a white man walking his child to elementary school.

There was a boycott in Lamar, a tiny town about 35 minutes northeast up Tobacco Road from Gamecock City, which was probably music to the ears of many Lamarites. It could've been *far* worse than a mere boycott. After all, this was the same town in tough little Darlington County where, just a few months earlier, citizens had overturned school buses in a veritable insurrection against desegregation. A mob of whites showed up with axe handles and other low-tech, but deadly, weapons and turned over two school buses taking black students to class. Meanwhile, at Cherryvale, a former plantation in Gamecock County where many slaves once worked the fields, white parents protested a lack of buses to get their kids to school. Irony atop irony.

In the midst of this mess, a lawyer at the United States Department of Health, Education, and Welfare's Office of Civil Rights told the Gamecock City District 17 Superintendent that he didn't care if *anyone* got an education – total desegregation must begin now! Or as the Supreme Court put it in *Griffin v. County School Board*, "The time for mere 'deliberate speed' has run out." Gamecock City's school administration felt the federal government's hot breath on its neck.

And so, the Class of '71's senior year was to be wild and wooly. But let me be clear. The Class of '71 had this mess *dumped* in its lap. The government could've chosen another forum in which to conduct this massive social change. It sure as heck could've gotten started sooner and planned things better. (Maybe the Freedom Riders crisscrossing Gamecock City a few years earlier might've given the government a heads up.) Instead, Congress and the South Carolina Legislature left it to the Class of '71 to dance this mess around. That's why the Class of '71's students (the *oldest* of whom were only 17 and 18 years old) and Gamecock City's school administrators were the ones who had to make it work. We didn't light the fire.

But hey, we also got to play football. Had a pretty good year, too.

CHAPTER TWO

The Many Faces of the South

Contrary to popular belief, there are many "Souths." Some are beautiful, some goofy, some angelic, and others evil. Most exist only in fantasyland, as do those God-awful fake Southern accents in Hollywood movies and television shows:

"Oh Ray-utt dahlin', let's just see-yuht hee-yuh and hi-yuhve a cold bay-uh on the end of my dahdee's dock."

I mean, come on.

Despite this fantasy, the South I've always known is something entirely unique.

The South of my youth was unlike the Gamecock City of today in at least a thousand different ways. Even folks' names back then were different. Southerners of my youth, white and black, tended to have Old Testament names – Malachi, Amos, Isaiah, Caleb, and Ezekial. African or Arabic names like Rashaad or Mahommed were rarer than a black Klansman. By the time I was in my 40s and teaching a first grade Sunday School class at Seacoast Church in Mount Pleasant, boys' names on attendance rolls were mainly right out of the New Testament – John, Paul, Matthew, Thomas, Mark, Timothy – things like that.

There also was the thing about going by initials. I don't how that came about. Maybe it was because presidents went by their initials (F.D.R. for President Franklin Delano Roosevelt and J.F.K. for John Fitzgerald Kennedy). Men of all backgrounds often used their initials instead of their first names. My grandfather was F.M. Moise, and my father signed his name R.B. Moise. Elvis' bass singer was J.D. Sumner. A buddy of mine in high school whose name was W.T. Hanna discovered that the South Carolina DMV had typed "W (only) T (only) Hanna" on his driver's license. We nicknamed him "Wonely Tonely."

Living was cheaper back then. The average yearly wage for Americans in those days was $3,851, and the minimum wage was a dollar an hour. Imagine that. Gas was about 23 cents per gallon, and the typical house cost about 11,000 bucks, which is pretty close to what my father paid for our house. Charleston's infamous Rainbow Row mansions were seen as white elephants, and they went for a song.

People always say that the South's pace is slow. I say that's a cliché. But if you think it's slow now, you should've seen it back in the day when the Class of '71 was young. Moise Insurance Service and many other Gamecock City businesses followed the English custom of shutting down at noon on Wednesdays. This allegedly dated back to England in the 1800s and compensated for the employees having to work on Saturdays.

Bankers had it good. Each day for a few hours at noon, Gamecock City's banks closed, thus the phrase "keeping bankers' hours." South Carolina's Blue Laws mandated that all stores close on Sunday, although necessities could still be sold by a few businesses. Except for private clubs, no beer, wine, or drinking alcohol was sold on Sunday either. That was okay because Gamecock City had little-to-no bars, though a few infested the outskirts of town.

With no megastores like Office Depot, Lowes, Publix, or even malls (Columbia's Richland Mall didn't open until 1961), many items had to be ordered through the United States Postal Service. No matter what the item was or from whence it would come, the thing always seemed to take two weeks to arrive.

In the countryside, my family's wall-mounted telephone was on a party line. This meant that anyone on our line, which included nosey neighbors, could listen to anyone else's conversation. (Imagine the drama.) Telephone numbers were mercifully short, which was good because most phones were rotary dialed, not push-button. Our home number was 33231. Neither area codes nor zip codes existed. All long-distance calls were done through a female operator, probably our class mother, Nancy Howle Patterson.

Despite growing up in Gamecock City, I wasn't born there. I was conceived and delivered just down the road in Bishopville, South Carolina, which is the seat of Lee County (named for the Confederacy's general, Robert E. Lee, who, in the 1950s, was tantamount to a saint among many conservative, white, local Southerners).

Soon after my birth, Momma was hot to trot outta Bishopville. She was suffocating in the tiny town and wanted the high life of a big city, i.e., Gamecock City. So, a few years later, with her thick blonde hair choked by a silk ribbon behind her neck, Mother downloaded my big brothers, Ben and Mike, my sister, Scott, and me, "The Kid," into a Detroit death machine. It was a black, steel-dashboard 1949 Ford sedan without seatbelts or effective safety glass.

Our dad drove us past white cotton and green tobacco fields through the infamous Scape Oar Swamp, a place we were told was the haunting ground of the "Lizard Man." We took Dead Man's Curve, a 90-degree turn, at 45 miles per hour and within a half hour, Daddy slowly rolled our car down the oak-lined boulevard into Ingleside, our home for the next four years.

Ingleside was my Grandfather Francis Marion Moise's farm on the Brewington Road in Gamecock County, not far from

Cubbage Road. I think we might've moved there because my dad couldn't afford to raise four (and eventually, five) kids on the salary he was receiving for writing "Not That It Matters," his newspaper column at *The Item*. My grandfather bought the place in 1920, an old plantation house replete with ancient slave cabins in the back, large, fertile fields, and a pecan orchard.

Turns out, we had moved to what Gamecock City's Chamber of Commerce was trying to sell as the "New South."

As for exactly what the "New South" actually meant? Well, that depended on who you asked and when you asked it. Generally speaking, it was often identified with progressive ideas, literary excellence, a business-friendly economic climate, and a turn away from the lynchings and oppression of blacks. "New Souths" sprout up erratically over the years, but there's not much doubt when the "Old South" supposedly died.

It was in the winter of 1865. That's when William Tecumseh "Cump" Sherman and the United States Army burned "Old Dixie" down. In 1865, they wreaked such utter destruction and mayhem that everyone, white folks and former slaves alike, had to recreate the South from its ashes.

Sherman left the women and children desperate. How desperate? Well, after General Sherman's soldiers had their fill of robbing and burning white Southerners' homes in Gamecock County, the mommas bided their time waiting for the cavalrymen to mount up and move to greener pastures. As the horse soldiers rode out of town, Southern women followed with containers. These women sought out the smoking fecal droppings that fell from the horses' anuses into the dusty dirt roads. From the hot horse feces, the women picked any corn kernels that hadn't been digested in the horses' stomachs, which they boiled to feed their children. That's how desperate. Cump Sherman would use the same brutal strategy on Native Americans after the Civil War.

His legacy lived and breathed for decades to come. There was no money to rebuild the South after the Civil War. In some ways, South Carolina was still feeling its effects until World War

II lifted the economic tide. My parents always scrunched up their faces in disgust at the mention of General Sherman as if he'd burned their *own* house or something.

Harper's Bazaar and other Northern periodicals back in 1865 were working overtime gloating about the tail whippin' that Southerners were getting. Yankee reporters didn't emphasize that women and children were left starving after Sherman's soldiers rolled through South Carolina destroying whatever crops and livestock the troops didn't steal.

Okay... so having brought up the subject of Yankees, let's just go ahead and get it right out in the open.

We're all Yankee Doodles now. From our armed forces fighting in Iraq to ranchers in Wyoming, and from union men and women in the steel towns to civil servants in Washington D.C., we're *all* Americans. Why a few Southerners take such pains to make visitors welcome but say ugly things about Yankees once they go back home is unclear. I have a theory though. Maybe it's because a tiny, inexplicable platoon of northern transplants and visitors insist on *provoking* Southerners to dislike them.

Take, for example, the gentleman who wrote a letter to the editor of the Charleston *Post and Courier* a while back. He was decidedly not gruntled. Apparently, one weekend morning during the sesquicentennial Civil War reenactment of the first shots fired at Fort Sumter, a cannon report woke him up. No cannonball was fired. One certainly didn't come through his *bedroom window* mind you. But it woke him up. Nonetheless, this rude awakening was unacceptable. He then proceeded to inform his neighbors of just how he felt about living amongst Southerners:

> "[W]hile I know what these people [(i.e., Southerners)] think of us, they should know what we think of them – we don't."

Well! Not getting invited to parties, are we?

So, that's the opinion of a few Yankees. I wonder: do Southerners act rudely when they visit up North? If so, they should be beheaded.

But listen, the South that Sherman burned down never actually died. In Gamecock City, we lived in a constant battle of "Us v. Them," which ultimately devolved down to black v. white. And why not? We were a 20th century town still living in the 1870s and fighting the battles of Reconstruction.

In 1958, slavery and segregation, the dominant social issues in modern American history, were a volcano about to erupt. Slavery had never been dealt with properly in the century since Reconstruction, and anyone with common sense should know that permanent segregation of an entire race is an inherently flawed concept, but blacks and whites seeing one another at work and walking the same streets was essentially the extent of racial interaction in 1958. Generally speaking, black and white citizens of Gamecock City existed on different planets. Segregation was the law, which meant different schools, different public-seating arrangements, and different water fountains. None of this seemed strange to my white friends or me. Segregation had been the law since our first newborn cries. We thought it had been there since the beginning of time.

I used to play war or army after school with my childhood buddies. Sometimes we were the United States Army fighting Germans. Other times, we were Confederates fighting Yankees. There was neither ideology nor logic behind our play. Nonetheless, nobody wanted to be either a German or a (ee-*yew*) Yankee, (except my cousin Billy whose dad was from Indianapolis). When I say "nobody," I just *assumed* that, across town, black kids wanted to be Confederates too, which shows you just how ignorant I was about that. But after all, how would I know?

Truthfully speakin', in the 1950s, many of us white children were so indoctrinated by our culture and history that we perceived Yankees and black people as inferior. It's sad to say, but that's the truth of it.

You might say that the Class of '71's childhood took place in that emotional valley between the peaks of World War II on one hand and the social revolution of the 1960s on the other. The parents' expectations about how we would turn out and our *own* plans for the future did not always connect. Soon, these same happy little tykes would wrap wicked frowns across their faces, spill onto Greene Street and into Maxcy Gregg Park in Columbia, and thrust angry signs at the police complaining about "the Man." "The Man," of course, was these same World War II veterans, the fathers and mothers, who bore and raised us. We baby boomers promptly reinvented ourselves as "the Counterculture," "the Movement," "the Love Generation," "the Cause," or whatever. The mass student protests we'd end up making about racial injustice, the bombing of Cambodia, the Kent State shootings, the Orangeburg Massacre, and other such social justice issues, had no precise precedents in American history. The closest parallels were the Civil War era abolitionists and suffragettes, and even those comparisons suffer.

The Class of '71 was comprised of baby boomers. However, I was a rather pitiful soldier for "the Cause." Other than our rock band, Wormwood, opening up on the Statehouse steps on Earth Day, 1972 for Allen Ginsberg to recite his poem *Howl*, my protesting was limited to throwing eggs at legislators' cars unlawfully parked around Columbia.

It was no surprise my generation took up the role of revolutionaries. Roughly speaking, the Class of '71 was the last generation in which the few remaining former slaves, Confederate soldiers, and the close descendants of each, lived together in the same cities. Just as important as the former slaves' presence was that of their children and grandchildren. They heard awful stories about rape, humiliation, and degradation on the plantations *directly* from their grandparents, great-grandparents, elderly aunts, and elderly uncles.

Each race inhabited its own little world. Theodore Adams was one of the first kids to integrate Orangeburg High School in the 1960s. In describing the interaction between black and white

11

folks before total desegregation, he said, "Up until the time when I went to Orangeburg High School my freshman year, I didn't *know* any white people. *Per*iod."

Didn't even *know* any white folks, for Lord's sake. This close proximity to the Civil War and slavery wasn't, as George Clinton of Parliament/Funkadelic might say, no theoretical thang. And the stories passed down weren't necessarily the same ones in sanitized books read secondhand in civics class these days. Explosive emotions stood in close proximity to one another. The Confederate States of America were real in the 1950s for us Gamecock Cityites, white and black. The CSA is a zephyr, always there, but so subtle you don't always notice it blowing.

Want another example? Take Arnold Murray. Although there was probably a debate about *who* actually was the last still-living Confederate veteran in the State of South Carolina when the Class of '71 was kids, a huge funeral was convened anyway for Private Arnold D. Murray at White House Methodist Church in Orangeburg. Many said that he was the last Confederate veteran in South Carolina, so what the heck, the State went with it.

A *huge* crowd, (approximately 5,000 people, according to the South Carolina Highway Patrol), showed up for the funeral. Both Governor James F. Byrnes and former Governor Strom Thurmond found time in their busy schedules to lead the funeral procession. Over a hundred of Pvt. Murray's family attended. Dixie was played, and the shots on Fort Sumter were reenacted by a group of Citadel Cadets. Private Murray had passed away just a few months before I was born.

Tell me the Old South wasn't alive and well when the Class of '71 came into being.

My point is this: slavery and the Civil War weren't ethereal concepts we saw on television or read about in books like King Arthur and his Knights of the Round Table. The cuts of former Confederate soldiers and their slaves still bled into the 1950s when the Class of '71 was born and maturing.

CHAPTER THREE

Gamecock City Through the Eyes of a Child

I grew up in a tight-knit community, and like many in the Class of '71, I was fortunate enough to be surrounded by a load of colorful characters starting early in my life.

One of my childhood friends since first grade was Leighton Cubbage. He has a number of nicknames, usually involving his head, including but not limited to "Big Cub," "Von Cub Head," "Cub Man," "Cabbage," and "Cabbage Head." I met Cub on the very first day of school at Central Elementary when my mother pointed him out to me in Miss Boney's classroom.

"Walk home with the boy with the big forehead," she said.

Cub wasn't hard to miss. He's always been several inches taller than me no matter what age we've been and a better athlete. Cub Man had dark curly hair (for a while) and cat eyes. He could charm girls to death with his unpredictable, self-assured personality. Cub lived in a white, two-story home at 125 Church Street. His house was just a block and three houses from where I lived on Church Street. The Cubbage residence was the only other home in Gamecock City where I could walk inside without knocking, open the refrigerator, pull out food, and start eating without suffering a speck of guilt for my bad manners. His parents, Ladson and Margaret Cubbage, always had smiles on their faces when I came by, which was pretty often.

My other early childhood buddy, Ned Parker, lived on Warren Court. As a boy, he went by his nickname, Nedro. We children were great proponents of sustainable, green energy at the time, eschewing motorized vehicles with toxic emissions in favor of bicycles. Ned lived just four minutes away via bicycle. Nedro was a good-lookin' boy about my height with undisciplined blonde hair. I'm not saying that he was fat as a young kid, but his favorite pet was a fried chicken. However, by the first day of football practice at McLaurin Junior High School, Nedro was all muscle, bone, and brains.

Truth be known, Nedro came from a different environment than Cub and I. My mother tried to emphasize education, being a teacher. It just never did much good with me until my third venture into college. In fact, my brothers and sisters and I were all pretty disinterested students until we got older. I don't recall Cub ever being chastised for bad grades by his parents. Maybe that's because he made flawless grades, but my recollection is that neither he nor I were obsessed with excellence in education. Nedro's entire family, however, was heavily into academic achievement. The Parker kids, all of them girls except Nedro, *killed* it in school. Nedro himself was Senior Class President. At the Edmunds High School Football Banquet in January of 1970, he was presented by Clerk of Court O.V. Player with the W.S. Jackson Scholastic Award. Coach Satterfield used to say that Parker "played smart" on the football field. Nedro was rewarded with a full ride to Yale. He turned it down, went to Davidson College pursuing a double major (pre-law and pre-med), then dropped out of college forever.

• • •

Our family home on Haynsworth Street was a brick house fronted by four white Corinthian columns rising two stories. Haynsworth Street was named after the infamous Gamecock City native, George Edward "Tuck" Haynsworth. Tuck had been a slight, mustachioed Citadel cadet. He was cursed with disappearing hair, against which he was fighting a rear-guard action in the form of a comb-over.

Tuck was the young man who, on April 12, 1860, supposedly pulled a cannon's lanyard to fire the first shot of the Civil War. He was aiming across Charleston Harbor at the *Star of the West*, a commercial steamer plowing toward Fort Sumter to resupply. It's unclear if Haynsworth actually *hit* the ship (the shot was supposed to be a warning fired across the *Star of the West*'s bow), but under the circumstances, it really didn't matter. The sentiment was pretty clear.

The wooden front porch of our brick house on Haynsworth Street was painted deep Charleston green, and two long black benches rested against the house on either side of the white trimmed front door. My dad, as frugal a man (I did not say "cheap") as I've ever seen, got a good deal on our home. A fifty-foot magnolia tree stretched languorously over the black iron sword fence bordering the front and side yards. Every spring, huge white flowers, nearly a foot across, sprouted on the magnolia's thickly barked branches. As any Southern boy who plays army knows, magnolia cones make wonderful grenades. The stem acts as a pin. Just break off the stem, throw the grenade straight-armed like a soldier, and *boom* – you've cleaned out a foxhole of Germans.

A wide concrete sidewalk marched directly from our front porch steps, through the sword gate, across the sidewalk, and out to the street. There, at the edge of the street was a carriage block. It was a solid square slab of white concrete that acted as a platform for visiting ladies and gentlemen. A lifetime ago, it helped them alight from their cabriolets and buggies to the sidewalk. Carriage blocks ornamented the sidewalks in front of our neighbors' houses too, although no horse had clopped down the street in over half a century.

My parents had five wacked-out kids to support, not to mention Belle, our Irish Setter, and a white cat, Jayo, named after the town drunk (my big brother Ben's idea). Mother always left at the crack of dawn to teach school then returned to take care of that house of rambunctious rascals.

Our family had a series of what we called "maids." They mainly watched us kids, cooked, and washed clothes. Most beloved of them all was Janet (pronounced Juh-NET) Addison, who raised us and covered for our transgressions when we were hauled before the court of parental discipline. Janet was an immaculately attired black woman. Her dresses were always splashed with lots of color. She was about 35-40 years old when she first took the job. She had no car. Instead, Janet caught a carpool ride each morning to Gamecock City from tiny Saint Charles, 19 miles away down Highway 401.

Whatever personal problems we children had (and there were many), Janet always listened patiently and never criticized. Several years after her employment, my father quietly bought her a frame home with a veranda in Gamecock City. Many years after that, when Janet died, my entire family drove from North and South Carolina to attend her funeral in a white, clapboard church in Lee County. Just thinking of her now makes me want to cry.

Another maid my family hired was a skinny white girl named Thomasina who filled in for Janet for a while. She looked to be about 16 years old, although she might have been as old as 19 or 20. Thomasina and I were not actually that far apart in age, but Sweet Jesus we were worlds apart in street smarts. By this, I mean that she had street smarts and I had none. Most days during her tenure as our maid, Thomasina was picked up after work in a maroon '58 DeSoto Sedan by a stocky man with a pompadour called Sampson. Sampson was maybe 45- to 50-years-old.

They were a real odd couple, although Sampson certainly was happy with the state of things. But one day, Sampson's Sedan stopped showing up in the afternoon when it was time for Thomasina to go home. The rumor was that Thomasina shot Sampson through the lip. The bullet having just missed Sampson's brain, he came out of the affair as healthy as a horse, free to live and love again. That was the rumor anyway.

After a while, we stopped seeing Thomasina, too. I liked her but had mixed feelings because I was shy and I thought she treated me very cavalierly. A young boy's self-confidence is often a pitifully fragile thing. Lord knows mine was. We all remember humiliating moments from our past that spring out of nowhere with a wince – a stupid remark we made or a dumb move like running into a door in front of a group of the opposite sex – and although the embarrassing thing lasts no more than a couple of seconds, our tender psyches are forever nailed against the tree of life by the terrible dart of shame. I assure you that I still do this stuff all the time. My specialty is walking out of a restroom into a room of women with my zipper wide open.

One of these moments happened to me with Thomasina when I was 11 years old. Thomasina barged inside my room in a sweat to clean it before she had to go home. Sampson was outside blowing the DeSoto horn. My bedroom door was cracked open, and she didn't bother to knock. She entered right in the split second between when I had just taken off my towel after a bath and before I had put on my tightey-whitey underwear. I was, as Southerners say, *buck nekkid* in front of a scornful 16-year-old girl. Thomasina wrinkled up her face and harrumphed. I was scarlet with humiliation, but Thomasina was unimpressed.

"Ain't nothin' but *hide*," she spat at me.

I was indignant and wanted to reply, but, honestly speaking, I was embarrassed with my shortcomings. I said nothing but remember it even today.

● ● ●

A couple of blocks away from us lived my Great-Great Aunt Penina. She lived in a white, two-story, wood-frame home of the Gilded Age with wide verandas and a brick walkway.

Aunt Nina had a lot going on. Even in her black, substantial pumps, she couldn't jump up and touch a five-foot doorknob. Aunt Nina's Coke bottle glasses? I think they were fake — she acted as blind as a newborn kitten, but got around her house just fine. She sometimes wore a dark visor of the type you'd expect to find on Bob Cratchit in *A Christmas Carol*. Aunt Nina was named after her aunt, the blind poetess and songstress Penina Moise. Aunt Nina's daddy, my great-great grandfather, was a Confederate cavalry officer, and her son, Rear Admiral Edward Alva Solomons, was Commander of Pearl Harbor.

I recall once, when I was seven, my father and I visited Aunt Nina. At the time she was 84 years old, and she received us in her upstairs bedroom.

"Come on in, y'all. I thought you'd left this old lady to die in solitude."

"No ma'am. No one would leave the crown jewel of Gamecock City to rust," Daddy replied obsequiously.

Aunt Nina always summoned her maid to bring out refreshments (sherry) for her and my father, which she claims was "prescribed by her doctor." Upon Daddy's instructions, I read *The Daily Item* to her. Even in her old age, her mind was as clear as a sunny morning, and she was just *crazy* about current affairs.

Let me tell you, I was bored *stiff* in Social Studies at McLaurin Junior High School, but Aunt Nina's stories about history were quite different. When she told us about how her father rode through maelstroms of Yankee Minié balls with Robert E. Lee's legendary Army of Northern Virginia, it made the Civil War as real as if it were happening that very day. Tales of how he was wounded fighting at Gettysburg and had three horses shot out from under him in a single day at the Battle of Butler's Tower near Petersburg excited me. She knew that he'd fought under Generals Longstreet, Fightin' Dick Anderson, Butler, and Hampton against the Army of the Potomac. Aunt

Nina told us how he and his high-testosterone cavalry jocks got into a fight with a federal gunboat near Smithfield in the James River, and after an excellent shot from nearby artillery, boarded the gunboat, and captured it.

Born nine years after the Civil War ended, Aunt Nina was just a young girl when soon-to-be Governor Wade Hampton and his Red Shirts cantered their sweating, high-strung horses outside her window in the tumultuous 1876 political campaign to take the state back from "carpetbaggers and scalawags." Wade Hampton is such a South Carolina icon that virtually every South Carolina town of any size currently has a Hampton Street.

On this particular visit, Aunt Nina's eyes glazed over at the thought of it: all those handsome young men. Her mother, Esther, would serve steaming soup to the Red Shirt militiamen from iron cauldrons suspended above oak fires in the emerald-green, grassy median of Warren Street.

When Aunt Nina spoke to me, the Civil War came alive, and I wanted to be a dashing cavalry officer. She didn't talk about slaves, probably because her daddy never owned any. Nor did she mention that some of those handsome young men in South Carolina's new Reconstruction legislature actually did bring some good ideas with them, not the least of which was the concept of free public education.

This was the culture in which the Class of '71 was raised. Some folks in our town derisively referred to Memorial Day as "Yankee Memorial Day." Instead of specifically observing "Yankee Memorial Day," many white members of the Class of '71 observed "Confederate Memorial Day," while simultaneously honoring veterans from the United States Armed Forces and the South Carolina militia. Our classes at Central Elementary School would line up at the blackboards and, led by our teachers, march outside to the granite Confederate Monument.

Each year on "Confederate Memorial Day" (at least until the early 1960s), my teeny-tiny Aunt Nina would lead a service honoring the Southern dead and those of the United States Armed Forces in most of America's other wars. The Confederate

Monument was an obelisk reaching to the sky above the school-yard, casting a long shadow over us wide-eyed children. There, standing in front of our school principal, the teachers, and the administrators, Aunt Nina would conduct a 15-minute program about the nobility of the Lost Cause. Many surnames chiseled onto that monument were identical to those of the little boys and girls standing beside me. The significance of the Confederate States of America would be reemphasized by many white parents around the supper table that night.

But it wasn't just in white people's memories that the Civil War still breathed. Former slaves, their children, and white folks brushed elbows on the streets of Gamecock City. They had *strong* opinions about Confederates and us white folks.

And Jim Crow? Well, he was everywhere and nowhere. He rode like a gargoyle in the passenger's seat of every deputy sheriff's police cruiser. Jim Crow's foul breath drifted forth like ancient dust from the South Carolina Code of Laws every time it was opened by a judge or prosecuting attorney.

While my Great-Great Aunt Nina loved to share stories of her daddy, my Uncle Nick, who worked a few blocks away along-side my father at his insurance business, had his own war stories to tell.

• • •

Uncle Nick, tall and sinewy with thick dark hair, was a born overachiever and quite aggressive by nature. When he spoke to me, he would get right in my face, make direct eye contact, and talk very loudly.

Nick was both an athletic and an academic star at Gamecock City High School. The superlatives continued at Duke University. He did well in his college classes and developed into a big man on campus. Nick made the Blue Devils' varsity swim team as a freshman. By his senior year, he was captain and the 1940 Southern Conference breaststroke champion.

Uncle Nick was matinee-idol handsome, in or out of his trendy, round Glenn Miller eyeglasses. He worked as a life-guard at the beach, where he probably did pretty well with the dames. Nick graduated Phi Beta Kappa in Economics in 1941 and went off to be inducted into the United States Army at Fort Jackson in Columbia. After suitable wooing while in basic training, Uncle Nick asked a dark-haired Jewish beauty, Cecile Rosenberg, to be his wife. She accepted and promptly converted to Presbyterianism, a family tradition. They married in cheesy Phenix City, Alabama (its founding fathers couldn't even spell the name right). Phenix City was a sin city, if there ever was one. Despite the short courtship, Nick and Cecile remained in love until death did them part.

The regular infantry was too pedestrian for Nick. He signed up for the paratroops. There are units in the American army, and then there are *legendary* units. Uncle Nick was in one of the latter, the famous 82nd Airborne with its AA shoulder patch signifying it as the "All American Division."

After basic training, Nick was convoyed in a troop carrier through German U-boat wolfpacks to England. From there, he parachuted 50 miles behind enemy lines in Operation Market Garden. Then, he and his buddies headed into camp at Suippes, France, a department of the Marne.

Soon thereafter, on December 17, 1944, some soldiers of the 82nd Airborne were in Reims partying in a French bar. Also par-tying in the same bar were paratroopers from the 101st Airborne, an equally famous division whose shoulder patch was a scream-ing eagle. Private first-class Edward Peniche, on the advice of a fellow 101st Airborne soldier who was irked at all the AA patches around him, threw a beer at a table of 82nd paratroopers. The beer hit a big paratrooper, who promptly walked over to the 101st table and inquired as to whom might have thrown it. A French tomato, perched at the table and lookin' for trouble, pointed at PFC Peniche. *Boom!* A riot broke out. They were still brawl-ing when they heard the MPs' whistles. But the whistling wasn't so much to stop the brawl as for another important reason: the quiet battlefront between the Allies and the Germans had just evaporated. The 82nd and 101st were rushed back to camp, then on to Bastogne where they were dumped directly in front of onrushing barbarians.

It was the Battle of the Bulge.

The Battle of the Bulge was, to say the least, a surprise to the 82nd Airborne. The Germans maniacally counterattacked Allied forces in northern France, Belgium, and Luxembourg. The thrust was so powerful that it caused a fifty-mile wide bulge in the American lines (thus its name). Allied leaders failed to notice until too late – partially because of bad flying weather (a.k.a. "Hitler weather") prohibiting Allied reconnaissance flights. The Fuhrer had brought up and hidden incredible numbers of men and war material right across from the Allied front lines.

In fact, Hitler attacked with more troops than he'd used to invade France in 1940 at the *start* of the war. The German Army and its tank divisions appeared out of nowhere. Hitler's most aggressive, ideological, blood-runneth-over Nazi tank commanders led the thrust. The Germans planned to drive to the coast where they would seize the Allies' petroleum stores and thus fuel Hitler's dying war effort. It was a do-or-die attack, Germany's last stand. The Allies were caught flat-footed, to say the least. No one really knew where exactly was the Wehrmacht. Major Dick Winters of the 101st Airborne's Easy Company wrote that, similar to the Duke of Wellington on the Eve of the Battle of Waterloo, his colonel arrived for battle in a dress uniform. He'd come directly from a wedding in England just as the company drove out of camp in trucks toward the overwhelming oncoming German Army. Entire American army units simply disappeared, chopped up and spit out before the German onslaught.

Once Eisenhower figured out what all the fuss was about and realized the seriousness of the attack, he reacted. One of the first things he did was to find the 82nd and 101st Airborne Divisions.

As for my Uncle Nick on that fateful night, he and his fellow 82nd Airborne paratroopers, (including Strom Thurmond, who'd

refused to take advantage of his draft exemption as a sitting circuit judge), climbed onto flatbed trucks and were rushed north
to the front through the placid, snowy countryside. Once there,
in powder two or three feet deep and wearing clothing inade-
quate for the frozen north of France, they were inserted directly
in front of the oncoming ocean of panzer tanks – waves and
waves of creaking heavy armor followed by determined infantry. Included were the 1st SS Panzer Division *Leibstandarte*; SS
Adolf Hitler; 2nd SS Panzer Division *Das Reich*; and the 9th SS
Panzer Division *Hohenstaufen*.

Unlike Hitler's Aryan supermen and wild-eyed ideologues,
the 82nd Airborne was comprised of gum-shoe Americans, citizen soldiers from places like Portland, New York, and Gamecock
City. But these American paratroopers, together with General
George Patton's Third Army, blunted the German thrust. Uncle
Nick's paratrooper division was hammered by German cannon
and mortar barrages so intense that American soldiers bounced
up and down in their foxholes.

The Allies won the Battle of the Bulge at the cost of 19,246
killed and 62,489 wounded. Each dead and wounded soldier was
the son of a mother and father. The war continued for a while.
Uncle Nick and his fellow soldiers in the 82nd pushed forward
toward Germany. They attacked and took a series of fortified
gun emplacements on the Rhine River.

They also took 150,000 German prisoners. Simply handling
the prisoners was beyond anything they'd imagined or for which
they'd been trained. Uncle Nick was awarded a Bronze Star,
among his other commendations, for all that fighting. He was
mustered out as a captain. The war left such a lasting impres-
sion on him that when he went back to France many years later
to tour the battlefields, he still had a tough time handling his
emotions.

Coincidentally, my Uncle Nick was not alone in his home-
town. Gamecock City housed not one, but many World War II
survivors at the same time.

• • •

Standing 5'6" tall (on a good day) with black hair, Abe Stern was a handsome young man who worked inside the aging wooden walls of Jack's Department Store in downtown Gamecock City. Although a grown man with a family, Abe and I were both unrepentant kids at heart. Abe and I loved to joke around, and we had both arrived in town around the same time (relatively speakin'). His most recognizable characteristics were his big smile and ready laugh. Once or twice a year, after school, I would go to Jack's Department Store where, at his invitation, I would unabashedly pull out my rusting Bundy student-edition cornet and play it for his customers.

Abe Stern's story starts out like a fairy tale. Long, long ago in faraway Poland, young Abe Stern, né Abraham Sztern, was a bouncing baby boy in a happy family home with five kids. The world was their oyster. Little Abe was born in Poland's third-largest city, Lódz (which means "boat" and is pronounced as "Woodge"), on the Bzura River. Lódz is smack dab in the middle of Germany's eastern border and Poland's greatest city, Warsaw. In the 1930s, Abe's daddy owned a small textile manu-facturing plant in Lódz. Workers wove cloth by hand there. The Sterns weren't rich by American standards, but they had meat on the table regularly. As a successful businessman, Abe's father was respected in town. When problems arose, his dad could help arbitrate the disagreements. Abe looked up to his father with the awe of a child.

Lódz is in East Prussia. Prussia is the military heart of Germany, home of the Teutonic Knights. Napoleon Bonaparte had given Lódz to the Duchy of Warsaw. When Hitler came to power, he saw East Prussia and Lódz as part of Germany Irredenta. In other words, Hitler believed that Lódz historically had been part of the German Reich, and he wanted it back.

So, Hitler made plans to invade Poland, and he entered into a secret pact with "Honest Joe" Stalin of the Soviet Union to divide up Poland between them. It was a pact between two devils, if there ever was one. If Abe's parents had any say so in the matter, they'd probably have gone with the Russian devil. Hitler agreed that the Soviet Union could occupy some of Poland. As part of the deal, Stalin agreed not to object *too* strenuously, if – only because of military necessity, of course – Germany just happened to invade Poland.

The Germans called this "military necessity" Operation Canned Goods. Sometime between August 17, 1939 and August 31, 1931, convicts were held under arrest in a schoolhouse in Oranienburg, Germany. Nazi SS soldiers showed up in Poland carrying Polish military uniforms. Twelve of the thirteen Polish prisoners were ordered to don the uniforms. After doing so, they were quickly injected with a deadly chemical. Then, the bodies were driven into a forest just ten miles west of Germany's border with Poland. There the bodies of the dead prisoners were arranged on the ground as if they'd just been in a firefight and shot. To an unknowing observer arriving at the scene, it would've appeared that Polish troops had invaded Germany and had been killed shortly after coming onto German soil.

The Germans then pretended to "discover" the bodies and brought in the press corps to get to the truth of the matter. They didn't. By this time, the lone surviving prisoner had been taken by SS men dressed in plainclothes to a nearby German radio station. A Nazi pretending to be a Polish patriot broadcasted a rousing call to arms against Germany. The faux-Polish patriot announced that Poland was invading Germany. The lone prisoner was then shot, right in front of a live radio microphone, by a brave SS trooper.

In the finest tradition of investigative journalism, the newspaper reporters quickly confirmed that the Polish military had attacked the *Vaterland*. Well, you might ask, did the world press wonder why Poland had invaded Germany (a military superpower) with only 13 Polish soldiers? Wouldn't the Poles have committed a bit more manpower to the invasion?

Whatever.

The next morning, Hitler declared war on Poland in retaliation.

In the ultimate understatement of the 20th century, all of this was about to shake up young Abe Stern's life forever. Not long thereafter, on September 8th, the massive German Tenth Army rolled into Lódz. The Poles retreated eastward, sure that military assistance from their bosom buddies (i.e., "allies") Great Britain and France, was right around the corner. Good luck with that. Meanwhile, the Soviets invaded westward into Poland to the Bug River. Many Jews lived in this area where the Soviets invaded. They were the lucky ones.

On May 1, 1940, Abe Stern and his family (along with other Jews) were rousted out of their homes in Lódz and relocated to Ghetto Litzmannstadt where, as German slaves, they manufactured bombs and other war material.

Life in the ghetto was oppressive for Abe and his family. Before being forced into Ghetto Litzmannstadt, the Sterns lived just a couple of blocks away from their home. Looking outside the ghetto's gates at their former neighborhood, it must've seemed like they'd have to wait a lifetime to get back there.

The Sterns bought a little drugstore in which to live, but as more Jews came into the ghetto, room had to be created for the newcomers. Sometimes twelve and fifteen people lived in a room and a half. Typhus hung over the district like a devouring fog. Tuberculosis ran through the ghetto streets with the immense rats scuttling about. No matter how bad things got in Ghetto Litzmannstadt, Jews never went to the local hospitals, according to Abe. Jews didn't return from German hospitals.

Everything in the ghetto was powered by humans because the Germans shut off the electricity. No gasoline or diesel-fueled machines were available for transportation or otherwise. Certainly, no horses graced the streets of Ghetto Litzmannstadt. Better known by their culinary name, "supper," horses didn't last long. Without sewerage facilities, the vast amounts of daily waste were just dumped in corners of the ghetto somewhere. Only about 20% of the Jews would survive. Little did Abe and his family know, but the ghetto was heavenly compared to their next destination.

On a warm day in the summer of 1944, the ghetto was evacuated. The Stern family, all still alive and relatively healthy, were ordered out of the ghetto with the other Jews. They were taken to the railway station and packed into boxcars standing straight up. The train began rolling to only God knew where. Shorter people without access to the air above them in the crowded boxcars suffocated and went into rigor mortis. Jews defecated and urinated where they stood. The Sterns traveled like this for three days without food or water (except the single water bucket allocated for the entire railcar).

Finally, on September 16, 1944, the locomotive scraped the rails to a stop. The railroad car opened. Lunging at 15-year-old Abe Stern's face were snarling maws of German Shepherds being held back by Hitler's screaming *SS Totenkopfverbände* ("Death Head Corps") troopers.

Welcome to Auschwitz.

Auschwitz was the largest of the Nazi camps. It was both a concentration camp and a death camp. A huge metropolis, at its peak it is estimated that between 900,000 and 1,135,000 people were burned, gassed, shot, starved, and/or beaten to death. The part of Auschwitz where the Sterns were sent was called Birkenau, also known as Auschwitz II.

Jews jumped down off the boxcar, and a line formed outside the train. When a Jew came to the head of the line, an SS trooper pointed right or left. Able-bodied workers went right. A few pretty girls and women might be sent to Auschwitz' brothel. The elderly and infirm were pointed left toward the block bathhouse, which actually was a gas chamber. Abe's mother was put to death instantly at Auschwitz-Birkenau. Incredibly, the three Stern daughters beat the odds at Auschwitz-Birkenau and were sent to a work camp in Czechoslovakia where they survived the war. His dad was sent to Dachau where he died. Lazer, Abe's brother, was later executed. It's said that his crime was sharing food.

Young Abe was sent to the slow-moving death line, the parade of death. It was the line to the Zyklon-B, cyanide-powered gas chambers. As his line shuffled slowly onward, a German soldier, for reasons only known to himself and God, pulled Abe Sztern aside and out of the death line.

It was a mixed blessing. Abe was now a citizen of the most awful dystopia in the history of the human race. It was as if every evil in the world had come to dance upon the thousands of defenseless victims who'd been assembled for their pleasure. From his striped-pajama uniform, Abe Stern saw it all – babies torn from screaming mothers' arms and smashed against walls, firing squads, lice, disease, starvation, rape, bodies stacked like lumber, and rooms of hair, artificial limbs, and shoes. The air was often wintry with human snow softly floating from the ovens.

After the initial processing, many SS troopers stayed at a distance from the Jews. Instead, the beatings and other abuses were done by tin gods called kapos, who were similar to prison trustees. These kapos were Abe's worst nightmare. Many kapos were ex-convicts who enjoyed humiliating prisoners. They were the law. Kapos could kill you just to break up the monotony.

Take, for example, August Adam. He was a sort of celebrity kapo at Mauthausen camp in Austria. A five-time convicted criminal, Kapo Adam carried a bat. He called it his "interpreter." Adam personally met the new inmates at the front gate because he wanted to select the professors, priests, judges, and lawyers. He showed them the green triangle on his shirt and explained that it meant he was a killer. Kapo Adam turned to the quivering men of a type who had once judged him and had towered so far above him in civilized society. He told them that things had changed:

> *"[H]ere, I am in charge. The world has turned upside down. Did you get that?"*

Auschwitz-Birkenau was terror, cold, starvation, deprivation, and threats by kapos every day. Some folks just said the heck with it, walked to the high-voltage electric wires on Auschwitz's barbed-wire fence, and grabbed them to get it over with. Abe and his brother were transferred from Auschwitz-Birkenau to a town called Stecken and finally to Camp Neuengamm in Ahlem, a town in Lower Saxony.

In Ahlem, Abe, still just a kid, was forced to work underground. It must've been a scene out of a subterranean-fiction novel, like Morlocks in *The Time Machine* or the slaves in *Metropolis*. At Ahlem, the Jews worked for a German company called Continental Gummi-Werke AG, which used German soldiers as guards. Abe and his fellow slaves cleared asphalt tunnels so that German tank and airplane parts could be made. It was killing two birds with one stone as far as the Nazis were concerned: they worked the Jews to death while the Jews help create war material to kill Amerikaners. Then, everything changed in an instant.

On April 10, 1945, Vernon Tott, a tall, blonde, happy-go-lucky infantryman and amateur photographer from Sioux City, Iowa, was in an American Army mechanized unit pushing toward Hannover with the 84th Infantry "Railsplitter" Division. Like Uncle Nick's 82nd Airborne, the 84th had just been through the same bitterly cold winter and lost a third of its troops in the Battle of the Bulge. Tott managed to get through it alive, as did his fellow soldier, Henry Kissinger.

As the 84th Division traveled toward Hanover, some of its soldiers were fooling around with a baseball. It was then that Tott heard screaming coming from a nearby road. It was from Jews inside the Ahlem concentration camp. The Jews had seen the baseball. Nazis didn't play baseball. The Jews figured the soldiers had to be Americans. The 84th Infantry had no clue what the shouting was about or that there was a slave camp down that road. Because the Allies were just now entering Germany, some in the 84th Division hadn't heard of concentration camps.

The GIs rolled their clinking Sherman tanks down the road to investigate. What they found was Abe Stern. The guards and kapos were gone. He had been hiding inside the rock quarry. What the Americans saw at the camp made them sick.

The camp was populated by wraiths and skeletons wearing masks of despair. The tough soldiers from the battle-hardened 84th Infantry Division were experienced dog faces – sad sacks who had fought from Belgium into Germany. But they didn't expect this. Some began to cry. Tott's black and white photos show the big American soldiers towering over the tiny, helpless Polish Jews of Hanover-Ahlem whom they've just rescued.

There were two classes of Jews inside Ahlem's fence: dead Jews, and the remaining 35 men just a few breaths short of death. Abe Stern was one of the latter. Many lay soaking in their own urine. The lice had not only infested their skin but had burrowed underneath it. Wretched, rotting bodies were piled up like fenceposts perfuming the place with the odor of death. Some photos of the dead in concentration camps showed naked bodies. Their clothes had been taken by the living.

When the Germans heard American guns approaching Hanover-Ahlem, the "healthy" prisoners were marched off by their SS overseers to the Bergen-Belsen death camp. In Hanover-Ahlem, a healthy Jew was a low threshold to meet, so you can imagine what was left. The pitiful remaining Jews were already turning the doorknob on death's door. The other prisoners called these poor souls "musselmen." Goners, in other words.

"Human beings are just—they can be beasts, really," says Abe Stern.

The Americans took Abe to a German hospital and instructed the doctors to treat him. You might imagine how Abe felt about Germans and their hospitals by this time. It took some time before the doctors could dig the lice out, but the medical staff healed him. Within about ten days or so, Abe Stern's health, *joie de vivre*, and sense of humor were returning.

Abe Stern had no job over here, but in the post-war confusion he managed to schlep over to the United States with two of his three sisters. At first, he lived in a dump in New York, worked a crappy job, and went to night school. He didn't care for New York, so he split town for California. After working in California as a shoe store clerk, Abe served his new nation in the United States Air Force. He was stationed at Shaw Field, Gamecock County, USA where he met his bride-to-be, Rachela ("Americanized" to Rhea), a pre-war Polish immigrant. Abe joined his father-in-law and wife's uncle in business, eventually coming to own Jack's Department Store. He became a United States citizen on March 21, 1952 in the federal courtroom of the Eastern District of South Carolina in Columbia.

By the time I met him in the 1950s, young Abe Stern was thriving. He and his wife were raising two children with plans for a third: Donna would become a teacher; Nat would graduate from Harvard Law School and is now a professor; and Sharon would become a school psychologist. Abe never played the victim or lost his happy demeanor.

• • •

I was fortunate enough to grow up in these fields of wisdom. The people that I knew from my childhood were ordinary, yet extraordinary, people. On top of those folks, Gamecock City housed some significant political and legal minds that contributed to the civil rights movement of the '60s and '70s. The Class of '71 grew up in these people's shadows: little did we know, but we weren't meant to be simple onlookers witnessing history, we were bound to make history ourselves.

CHAPTER FOUR

The Political and Legal Powers of Desegregation

When the United States Senator from South Carolina, Burnet Rhett Maybank, died suddenly in office in 1954, Strom Thurmond became a young rising star in the Senate alongside Olin Johnston. Then, Fritz Hollings took Johnston's Senate seat in 1966. Once Thurmond and Hollings got their feet inside the Senate door, you couldn't run 'em off with a stick. Hollings was still there 39 years later. Strom lasted 48 years.

Senators Thurmond and Hollings. Now *that* was a pair. Both were masterful public speakers, though they used different styles. Strom Thurmond could raise the roof like a Pentecostal minister. He learned his style from an occasion on which he watched two stump speakers orate to a crowd. One speaker, a judge, approached the debate with quiet logic and reason. The other one was a politician with half the judge's intellect who jumped up and raised Cain, rabble-rousing the crowd until they were on his side. The rabble rouser ate the judge's lunch and won the election. Thurmond promised himself that no one would take advantage of him that way.

Hollings had a laid-back style that could be equally funny and charming. One clear afternoon in November of 1988, our law firm, Grimball and Cabaniss, was walking to our traditional Friday lunch and stumbled upon the renaming ceremony for the Hollings Judicial Center (now renamed again as the J. Waties Waring Judicial Center). According to Hollings, so many buildings had been named after Thurmond that there was a need to name a building after him for proper balance. But that was his sense of humor.

We stopped and stood in the press of Charleston lawyers, local news crews, politicians, and hoi polloi. A platform had been set up in the middle of Meeting Street where the bigshots, including Chief Justice William Rehnquist, were seated. Senator Thurmond spoke first. Even though Thurmond was closing in on 90 years of age at the time, he practically levitated off the platform in his enthusiasm, shaking his fist and pointing an angry finger at nobody in particular. Senator Hollings, Queen for a Day with his own judicial center being dedicated and all, spoke last. Hollings told a story about how he was recently in his Washington D.C. office when a voter from Greenville County burst in.

"Senatuh! Senatuh!" cried the man. "You gotta get down to Graaaaainvul. They tellin' all *kina* lies 'bout you down they."

"No main," Hollings said. "I gotta get down to Chawellston where they tellin' da *troot* 'bout me!"

The *troot* was that Senator Hollings was only one of eleven senators who had voted against Thurgood Marshall to be the first black Justice of the United States Supreme Court. But nobody came out of that battle unsullied. After all, in the 1950s and 1960s, civil rights weren't a problem. Not for white folk anyway. The civil rights movement in Gamecock City (or across South Carolina, for that matter) didn't really have a noticeable impact on the Class of '71's daily lives until the 1960s. But it was only a matter of time before dinner would be served.

It was like making grits. The ingredients were already in the pot – salt, pepper, corn meal, butter, and water. Someone just needed to light the stove. Laws had changed in Washington. Young, hungry, civil rights attorneys were coming of age. The will to enforce constitutional rights for blacks was coalescing, and a focal point was in Gamecock County and Clarendon County next door.

• • •

The power structure in Gamecock City, like the rest of the state, was exclusively white in the 1950s. You could drop a bomb on the city and not hit a black elected official.

Black people really hadn't had any say in South Carolina government before that, except during Reconstruction and for a while thereafter. And whatever rights they still had after those few decades evaporated overnight when one-eyed Ben "Pitchfork" Tillman used his political muscle to push through a new state constitution. It was reminiscent of Reich Chancellor Adolph Hitler's signatures on the Nazi Nuremburg laws in 1935. On November 13, 1935, Jews were German citizens and could vote. The next day, they weren't and couldn't. On December 3, 1895, black South Carolinians were relatively free under the law. The next morning, segregation was the law. Ole Pitchfork had seen to that. And so it remained until the Class of '71 was in our respective elementary schools.

Even when segregation was technically officially struck down, it really wasn't. Only about 20 percent of blacks were registered to vote when the 1957 Civil Rights Act was proposed. Due to the constant watering down and amending of the Act, even fewer Southern blacks were voting by 1960.

Black folks usually didn't make it onto juries either. In South Carolina, they were excluded either by law, by the clerks of court, or through lawyers' jury strikes. A few lawyers still alive today can remember the federal clerk of court actively excluding blacks from the jury venires, as well as union members and poor people so that trial jurors tended to be white property owners.

Joe Cabaniss, who taught me how to be a lawyer, used to tell a story about a black juror who was summoned to court for jury duty in the 1950s. The federal clerk of court in Charleston made up the jury list as usual, and based on these lists, summonses for potential jurors had been issued. A black juror named Whaley actually made it onto the venire. How did *that* happen? The clerk was confronted by a trial lawyer with this travesty. The clerk strenuously defended himself, explaining that he thought the juror was a white relative of Ben Scott Whaley, a legendary white Charleston trial lawyer. He had not considered that the juror's ancestors might've been the *property* of Ben Scott Whaley's ancestors or relatives. Not until 1986, when the United States Supreme Court decided *Batson v. Kentucky*, did it become unconstitutional to strike jurors on the basis of race.

In our youth, black lawyers were as rare as black elected officials. To say the least, there weren't many in Gamecock City. The NAACP held its annual meeting in Spartanburg, South Carolina, and Gamecock County only had three lawyers in the house: William B. James, a well-attired, bespectacled man; Esau Parker, publisher of *The People's Informer* (slightly taller than James and also well-dressed with a serious look about him); and finally, Ernest J. Finney, Jr.

James and Parker, however, stopped practicing in Gamecock City in 1954. Finney stayed. He would become legendary as the first black Chief Justice of South Carolina's Supreme Court. He made Gamecock City his home and helped desegregate it. Chief Justice Donald W. Beaty of Orangeburg now presides as the second black Chief Justice in South Carolina's history.

One of Finney's initial experiences with the South Carolina Bar wasn't as a lawyer. When the Bar Convention was held at the Ocean Forest Hotel in Myrtle Beach, he was serving food as a waiter. Apparently, this is good training to be a Chief Justice:

Rehnquist also worked lifting trays as a student worker in the Stanford Law School cafeteria.

And as for the black judges of our youth? There were none. No living lawyer had ever been into a Gamecock City circuit courtroom where a black judge was on the bench. It wasn't until after 1980, when Richard Fields of Charleston (Howard University, School of Law '49) was elected to the circuit bench, that a black judge was even eligible to preside in Gamecock County. (On a prior visit to Orangeburg County to search titles, the clerk of court made him use the janitor's restroom.)

Trust me, Judge Fields was the perfect lawyer to break that glass ceiling. Short and handsome with huge eyeglasses, a manicured moustache, and a million-dollar smile, Judge Fields was a pleasure to appear before. He was a lawyer's judge, meaning that he knew the law, let attorneys try their cases without buttin' in, gave reasonable continuances for trials if the attorneys had a problem finding witnesses, and didn't ridicule them in front of their clients. Moreover, he was pleasant and liked to keep the atmosphere upbeat.

There were no women in the Gamecock City Bar either, although Governor Richard I. Manning III of Gamecock City *had* signed a statute on February 14, 1918 allowing women to practice law. The official Gamecock City Bar photos of the 1950s and 1960s showed only graveyard-serious white Christian and Jewish men. They were a tough bunch of mugs.

The Law in Gamecock County during my youth was Sheriff I. Byrd Parnell. He could throw a black man in the Gamecock County Jail just for sitting at a lunch counter at a white business. Black folks weren't allowed back then to shop at many white stores or sit at white lunch counters. (Who came up with *this* business model?)

Law enforcement officers like Parnell had their hands full with this desegregation law. In October of 1963, when most of the Class of '71 was just 10-years-old, sit-ins were staged by black citizens in Gamecock City at Lawson's Pharmacy, S.H. Kress, Mitchell's Drugstore, Rowe's Drugstore, and Cut-Rate

Drug Store. This caught President John F. Kennedy's attention. Ernest Finney traveled to Washington, D.C. at the President's request to talk about the treatment of the protesters at Gamecock City's sit-ins. While Finney was in Washington, more arrests were made in Gamecock City, including those of Gamecock City blacks who'd been taken into custody for protesting at the local drive-in theater.

These arrests stressed the capacity of Gamecock County's jail, especially when incarcerated protesters refused to pay their fines. This all occurred on the same day. You'd almost think that it was planned in advance.

Black students from Morris College staged sit-ins at local lunch counters on several occasions in the early 1960s. There had been freedom riders in-and-out of Gamecock City over the years, and the United States Supreme Court was keeping steady pressure on Southern school boards to totally desegregate their classrooms.

Racial tension surrounding segregation was blossoming at the same time that the Class of '71 began attending public schools. Although we were just kids, we were exposed to these tensions and were aware that something was happening; we might not have known exactly *what* was happening, but even the most innocent of humanity could feel the wheels of history turning. I personally was exposed to these protests on November 20, 1960, a seemingly ordinary Sunday morning at the First Presbyterian Church.

CHAPTER FIVE

Protest and Politics – The Tension Brews

The First Presbyterian Church is a large building of white-painted brick on the corner of Main and Calhoun Streets in the heart of Gamecock City. Like most second graders in the Class of '71, I was unaware at the time that as Dr. McLeod stood inside preaching the gospel in his low-key way, four young Morris College students appeared outside. They were walking up the steps to the front door in anticipation of doing a kneel-in. An usher, working the front-door detail that day, intercepted the students and refused to allow them entry.

The usher was asked by the students whether it was not true that the black and white races serve the same God. The usher told them, and I paraphrase, that they had their own stinkin' church and to go there and worship, aye? To my knowledge, it was the first time in Gamecock City's history that anyone tried to desegregate a church.

The news wires burned red hot reporting this clear violation of the "What Would Jesus Do" rule. The church later contacted the same students through the school board's superintendent, Dr. Laurin McArthur, and asked them to return the next Sunday to perform their kneel-in, which they did.

The First Presbyterian Church hadn't always behaved this way. The church had clearly forgotten its own legacy of goodwill. With the help of a Yankee minister who had made his way in a one-horse gig down to tiny Gamecock City through rain and ruts, the First Presbyterian Church had been organized on May 29, 1823. The *first* new member received by the Presbyterians was a black woman named "Milly." The Session, "having obtained satisfactory evidence of her personal piety, voted unanimously to receive her." Milly, plus the five organizers, made a total of six people comprising the church. That was over four decades before Union General Potter's troops marched down Main Street and even longer before Ben Tillman pushed through South Carolina's Jim Crow Constitution. A whole lot of water had flowed past Sumter's Landing since then, and I suspect Milly had been forgotten by 1960.

Gamecock City and small towns like it across America in the 1960s were on two-year social delays from the rest of the United States' mindset. When the "Death of the Hippie" was proclaimed on October 6, 1967 by a group of long-haired pseudo-mourners in San Francisco's Golden Gate Park, hippies had barely shown up in Gamecock City. But by 1970, new politics and attitudes had certainly infiltrated Gamecock City. Revolutionary chic fashion was part of this. For example, in the early 1960s, some black students favored short-cropped hair or a "process," the latter of which was a chemically straightened hairdo. Processed hair was said to be "fried, dyed, and laid on the side." It was not a great time for fashion. Nobody, white or black, looked real good, despite what we might've thought.

The process hairdo yielded to huge, frizzed-out Afro-Sheen hairdos. Afros had debuted in America when P.T. Barnum, a notoriously racist showman, took the legendary Circassian beauties from the Northern Caucasus on tour in the 1800s; by the late 1960s, afros were reclaimed and making a comeback, but this time in a revolutionary capacity. They became the coiffure of choice by black-power radicals Stokely Carmichael, Malcolm X, and Angela Davis. An afro could increase the wearer's height by as much as four inches or more and was often sported in conjunction with sideburns and a goatee by men or huge loop earrings by women. The afro was a powerful political symbol of racial pride.

Another new political attitude that swept through Gamecock City with afros in 1970 was the radical notion of school desegregation. There was understandably a more strident tone appearing in black students' voices. After all, some Jim Crow laws were still being enforced even though they had been struck down by the United States Supreme Court. By 1970, white boys and girls alike were also tuning into the "revolution."

• • •

By the end of the Class of '71's junior year, there were only two public high schools in Gamecock City's District 17. One was Edmunds High School, 98 percent white, whose mascot was a Gamecock. The mascot was chosen for two reasons. It was named after Revolutionary War General Thomas Sumter (the "Fighting Gamecock"), and the Gamecock was the mascot of South Carolina's best-funded state college, the University of South Carolina. The other high school in Gamecock City was Lincoln High School, an urban Rosenwald school.

So what was a Rosenwald School?

After Reconstruction, Gamecock County had built thirteen Rosenwald schools, which, for the first time, had given local black children in some rural areas a fighting chance for an education. Rosenwald schools were found in all parts of the South, rural and urban, but they were particularly significant for rural communities because educational facilities of the time were particularly unfunded. These Rosenwald schools were more than just a place to teach kids. They also functioned as community centers and farm-education classrooms. Occasionally, several houses were built around a Rosenwald school, and the area would become a distinctive settlement or town in its own right.

Rosenwald Schools were the gifts of Julius Rosenwald, who was President of Sears, Roebuck, and Company. Basically, he was the Jeff Bezos and Amazon.com of the day. Pictures of him from the early 20th century show a short, dapper, mustachioed man wearing a black Homburg hat and an expensive business suit.

The man was a business genius. When free postal delivery to rural America was instituted in 1896, Rosenwald came up with a groundbreaking idea: mail-order shopping. Sears catalogues allowed country people to order a wide range of clothes, guns, kitchen products, and whatever else someone wanted through the mail or by rail. Sears even shipped houses in kit form that were assembled on the spot (one of them is found today south of Broad Street in downtown Charleston). Sears catalogues were the dream books of many Class of '71 members. They were discontinued in 1993.

Rosenwald's bright idea made him fabulously rich, and with his newfound wealth, he became a philanthropist, basically the Andrew Carnegie of black student education in the South. Rosenwald teamed up with another educational giant, Booker T. Washington, and together they came up with a way to encourage the creation of black schools in the South: if black folks could accumulate enough money for the mission through fundraising and soliciting contributions from local governments, Rosenwald would chip in for a significant portion of the start-up costs. The only other requirement was that once a school was built, the local government had to agree to incorporate it into the existing school system.

Like the Sears kit houses, Rosenwald had architects draw up state-of-the-art building plans, which ranged from one-teacher schoolhouses up to seven-teacher brick buildings with privies and teachers' cottages included. Often constructed in the countryside, many of the Rosenwald schools lacked electricity, so the classrooms were designed with large, strategically placed windows to let in significant sunlight. Everything was planned right down to the high ceilings, desks, blackboard locations, and paint colors. But as the state became desegregated and the legislature devoted more money toward black schools in an attempt to avoid total desegregation, the Rosenwald schools were abandoned (another example of the Law of Unintended Consequences).

• • •

Of the two campuses, Lincoln had a far longer history. Lincoln Grade School was built on Council Street in 1874 to educate all of Gamecock City's black students. Edmunds High School wasn't opened until 65 years later in 1939 when the white boys' and girls' high schools were consolidated into a building on Haynsworth Street. The white and black high schools were like South Sea islands – separate and apart unto themselves. They were easy walking distances from one another, but they might as well have been on different continents. And in many ways, they still were.

Sports games were never played between Lincoln High School and Edmunds High School. No reason to upset the applecart, aye? Then again, the University of South Carolina Gamecocks didn't play the South Carolina State College Bulldogs either.

The separate and discrete existence of these two segregated schools was undoubtedly fueled by many significant reasons, but one stands out. It was the same reason Tevye sang of in *Fiddler on the Roof*: "Traditionnnn, tradition!" Generations of black and white folk had been educated at those separate institutions, and there was one thing both schools shared equally – their own, special time-honored traditions.

Grandfathers, fathers, big brothers, cousins, uncles, you name it, had played football and basketball on the Lincoln High teams and wanted their children to follow in their footsteps. Mothers and fathers couldn't wait to sit in the stands, especially on Parents' Night, to see their sons and grandsons wearing Lincoln High colors beating up on some other high school. Say what you would about the Bulldogs, but they were tough. A few years before the schools were totally desegregated, a Lincoln guard named Artis Rucker had played both offense and defense – on a prosthetic leg. Like the white school not far away, the Lincoln students had their own boring alma mater ("O Lincoln High, hail! hail! to thee we pray!") that they mumbled and stumbled through. For many black and white families at that time, graduation from high school marked the end of their formal education, the last school they'd ever attend. They wanted that school to be Lincoln High.

Lincoln High School was a busy place in the spring of 1970. There were literary publications in the works, including the *Quill and Scroll* and the *Echo*. Each had an ambitious student editorial board already working on next year's edition. Its yearbook, *The Lincolnite*, was in the planning stage. More telling were *The Lincolnite*'s student pictures, where dark glasses, goatees, and afros were popping up. The revolution was in motion.

Its faculty and administrators enjoyed the great prestige and accouterments of respect and seniority after decades of public service. Who needed competition from white teachers five or six blocks away across town? Compared to other black schools, the Lincoln faculty had done a pretty good job. In fact, Lincoln sometimes sent over half of its grads to institutions of higher education compared with the national average of only three percent. So long as things remained the same, there was neither danger of Lincoln's teachers nor students being robbed of their professional status or larceny of their hard-earned perquisites.

Certainly, when it came to choosing who would teach what and where after total desegregation, the black teachers and athletic coaches felt they were as equally qualified as the white faculty and administrators to chair, for example, a mathematics or social studies department or lead a football team.

Similarly, at Edmunds High School, the mainly white student body was also happy with business as usual. They were coming off a legendary year in which Edmunds High's student body got extraordinarily high marks for academic excellence in statewide competitions. The football team had just won the state 4-AAAA football championship in an undefeated season (and one that has never been equaled for that matter). The school also won the state track 4-AAAA championship, and the Gamecock band had even won second place in statewide competition. For Edmunds High School, this had been a golden age of academics, music, and athletics.

Like the editor and staff of *The Lincolnite*, the rising editorial staff and faculty advisor were planning their 1971 *Hi-Ways* yearbook. Club officers had already been named. For the 12th Graders at Edmunds High School, this was not going to be just *any* year. It was *the* year, the much-anticipated *senior* year. Many of us believed that this was to be the penultimate time of our youth.

• • •

Dr. Laurin McArthur was Superintendent of Gamecock City's District 17 schools where I attended. A thin, greying, handsome, and well-spoken war veteran, he had earned a Bronze Star in the Battle of Leyte Gulf, likely the greatest naval battle of World War II and possibly in history. The sea and sky were aflame for days as airplanes and massive ships attacked several Japanese strike forces, and vice versa. I doubt that many, or any (outside of his children), students knew that he'd been in harm's way because, like most of the men and women returning from war, he didn't talk about it. Maybe he should've. It would've impressed me, that's for sure. Could anyone have handled the impending explosion of school desegregation? Well, he had a good shot at it. And he did handle it – maybe not perfectly – but as best he could with a conservative school board looking over his shoulder.

A taste of what was to come took place at Edmunds High's last graduation ceremony on June 1, 1970. As the Gamecock City High School Class of 1971 (i.e., us) watched, there was a deviation from the script. Several students, possibly including Mike Heriot, a basketball player, Charles ("Chuck") Heyward (soon to become a DJ at WWDM ("The Big DM") radio station), and John Pressley, a star on our state-championship football team, gave the black power symbol (raising a fist into the air), instead of shaking the hand of Dr. McArthur, when receiving their diplomas.

"[T]he incident left me more badly shaken than any other in my entire life," Dr. McArthur wrote in *The Pleasure of Remembering What Schools Can Do in South Carolina*. "Auto wrecks and World War II battles were nothing compared to this."

Just as my grandfather, a white Lee County cotton farmer, refused to shake hands with a black man back in the 1940s and 1950s, a generation later, two black men refused to shake hands with a white school superintendent.

After the exchange with the black students, McArthur promptly put the diplomas behind the lectern, and they walked off un-diplomaed. The audience of largely white folks gave a standing ovation to McArthur. Then, one of the more resourceful black students snatched the diplomas and allegedly burned them while sitting in his seat among the other graduates. And just like that, the Class of '71 inherited the title of "seniors."

CHAPTER SIX

The Summer of '70

There's a time called *Rumspringa* in the lives of Amish teenagers. It literally means "running around." Until they turn 16 years old, Amish boys and girls live under strict control of their parents and their church. They look, act, and carry themselves like the traditional Amish kids we see on television and in movies, but in their 16th year – boom! Amish parents turn the boys and girls loose to socialize, explore the real world of the "English" (i.e., us), and possibly to meet their future spouses. Amish children usually don't attend public school past the 8th grade, so they enter the workforce early.

On *Rumspringa*, they're given extraordinary freedom for such previously sheltered kids.

In the surrounding communities, local degenerates closely watch these unworldly-wise kids leave Amish territory. They're like crocodiles silently watching wobbly-kneed, baby wildebeests slide down African riverbanks for their first drinks of water. Amish boys dance shirtless around a campfire with Smirnoff vodka shooters in the back pockets of their blue jeans. The same virginal Amish teenage girls, seen by day in black, handmade dresses and prim white cotton hats, now spend their evenings in truck beds of jacked-up, mufflerless F-150s wearing tight skirts and midriff-exposing shirts with henna tattoos on their arms.

Down in Gamecock City, South Carolina, a few months before school began our senior year, it just so happened that I was in the midst of a laid-back *Rumspringa* of sorts myself. Time was cheap and life was sweet at seventeen. Everything I did was late: I fell into bed late, I rolled out of bed late, usually anytime between 9:30 a.m. and noon. I hadn't made my bed since the 6th grade. I was utterly useless. There had been little progress on my part since the umbilical cord was cut. Like most 17-year-olds, I thought my parents were boring, and I was sure that I knew everything. Of course, the reality was that I was the boring one, and my parents knew pretty much everything worth knowing. My father had sailed most of the way around the globe in harm's way. Me? I was just a skinny, 5-foot-10-inch tall boy with dark hair, an unreliable complexion, a large, unwieldy snout, and a love of the "Bullwinkle and Rocky Television Show." I didn't even know exactly where I'd be going to school in a few months. Our new unitary, integrated school system was still being hastily assembled pursuant to an agreement with the United States Health, Education, and Welfare's Office for Civil Rights. It wouldn't really exist for a month or two. The concept of a "new school" didn't bother me – I knew it would have a football team. That's all I cared about. I was sorry that so many of my friends were transferring to private schools (about 10 percent of the class) such as Wilson Hall and Thomas Sumter Academy, but I didn't waste a second worrying over that.

Scott, my pretty, blonde sister, named after her great-grandmother Elizabeth Scott, was in Gamecock City on sabbatical again from the "Party School" (as the University of South Carolina was called). She was back home in Gamecock City "finding herself." In other words, Scott had been kicked out of college for failure to meet the University of South Carolina's stringent academic requirements (a 2.0 average at the time).

Scott imagined herself as part Della Street and part TV attorney Perry Mason. Perry Mason excited her admiration for all things legal. *My Life in Court*, an autobiographical paperback book of short stories by famous New York trial attorney Louis Nizer, sat on her bedside table.

My two big brothers, whom I looked up to, were both married and out of the house. Ben, my oldest brother, never played by the rules. He was busted once for stealing a truckload of watermelons expropriated from a local sharecropper. Ben's free spirit earned him a stint at Carlisle Military School in Bamburg. There, Ben was beaten into submission on his first day when he refused to clean an upperclassman's shoes. From Carlisle, he did a stint at the Citadel, the military college in South Carolina.

Ben was always quite creative. He loved to paint and write. A macabre short story he wrote was published in *The Shako,* the Corps of Cadets' student literary arts magazine. Despite his literary inclination, Ben was not exactly obsessed with making great grades at the Citadel. The day his freshman grades arrived in the mail, Ben opened the transcript and handed it to our father, who was paying for Ben's education. Dad looked eagerly at the grades and immediately wished he hadn't. Ben had achieved Fs in four subjects and a D in the remaining one. Daddy sat in silence for a bit and then said, "Ben...I think you're spendin' too much time on one subject."

When Ben's belle, Anne Miller, graduated from Ashley Hall, the all-girls college preparatory school in Charleston, and enrolled in the University of South Carolina, Ben transferred to Columbia, too. Unlike my sister Scott, Ben was able to meet the University of South Carolina's rigorous 2.0 GPA requirement. However, Statistics was always his downfall. He couldn't get his bachelor's degree until he passed it; Ben took it over and over but never succeeded. For a time, he and my brother Mike worked as orderlies at the South Carolina Lunatic Asylum, as it was called in those days. Eventually, Ben joined the Coast Guard, converted to Judaism, unconverted, then converted to Buddhism, and got assigned to the *Paw Paw*, a cutter in New Jersey. Dad and Mom occasionally got letters from him (asking for money, I bet).

In 1970, my middle big brother, Mike, was back in Gamecock City from South America. He lived in a white, one-story house owned by my uncle on Hampton Street. Mike had previously joined the Air Force, and by a stroke of extraordinarily good luck, he had been assigned as an observer in Surinam. This was at a time when most folks who were drafted or enlisted were given one-way passes to Vietnam. Surinam is on the northeastern coast of South America and is famous for its cockroach. Mike didn't even have to wear a uniform in Surinam.

Since my earliest recollection, it'd been impossible for me to live up to Mike's reputation in Gamecock City. A good-looking blonde-haired guy reminiscent of movie star Tab Hunter, he had beautiful girlfriends that he'd bring home and for whom I always developed instantaneous crushes. In high school, Mike was a star offensive end on the football team. Imprinted in my memory is his picture on the front page of *The Gamecock City News'* Saturday sports section. He was reaching for a touchdown pass. I wanted to be a star pass receiver just like him. Unfortunately, he had hands of gold, and I had hands of Swiss cheese, full of holes. In the family tradition, Mike had been summarily booted from the University of South Carolina for bad grades, which is why he'd wound up in Surinam in the first place.

Roo, my baby sister, was an eighth grader at McLaurin Junior High that summer. Roo's nickname arises from her Christian name "Claire," the mellifluous French word for clear. "Claire" was extended into Claireroo, then hacked into Roo. Just like her name, Roo, was a pretty young junior high school girl. She had the thick brown hair of a Breck shampoo model, Margaux Hemingway eyebrows, and a cute pug nose like her mother. Claire was just beginning to innocently recognize and revel in her own femininity, always talking with her girlfriends, especially Cousin Margaret Harritt, about boys and what they were going to wear to school the next day. Eventually, Roo's muliebrity got the better of her. For her transgressions, Roo was quietly banished to Ashley Hall in Charleston where the path to righteousness was more clearly defined.

These were supposed to be the last 12 months I'd ever live in Gamecock City. Similarly, it was the end of childhood for most of the Class of '71, although truthfully speaking, our childhood has never ended. Well, not yet anyway.

Change was amongst us. Soul music, oxford shirts, and oxblood Weejuns penny loafers were disappearing from the streets of Gamecock City every day. It was as if the 1960s were burning rubber in a Chevelle V-8 Super Sport on Highway 15 South leaving town toward Paxville. At the same moment, the 1970s were rollin' into town on Highway 15 North inside a Volkswagen van painted with slogans of peace, love, and daisies.

The ministers and Sunday School teachers had told us to be on the lookout for an infiltration of agent provocateurs into Gamecock City. And surely enough, they came in a steady stream. They were mostly comprised of those humanistic Shaw Air Force Base military kids. They were smoking pot, wearing love beads, and tie-dying their t-shirts. By 1970, however, the Class of '71 itself was starting to revel in the bacchanalia of the hippie movement like pigs in mud holes. A little late, but getting there.

After all, the prior summer had seen the ultimate moment of peace, love, and music, better known as Woodstock. Despite the fact that roughly 400,000 people showed up for the event in New York, the Woodstock generation was not universally approved of. George Meany, AFL-CIO Founder and President, commented on the distaste, saying, "If the younger generation are the hundred thousand kids that lay around a field up in Woodstock, New York, I am not going to trust the destiny of this country to that group." Then again, his name was Meany, so what do you expect?

"Southern grits," was what the hippie wannabes called straight and narrow people like most of us in the Class of '71. Head shops sprang up like little white lawn mushrooms after a heavy rain.

OK. I suppose I was a Southern grit. My main activity in the summer of '70 was playing a Farfisa Mini Compact organ in a nine-piece horn band called The Tempests. Our business card read: "The Tempests, Rhythm and Blues."

The epicenter of social life in the 1960s was a quaint little wooden rec center called the "Teenage Canteen," where The Tempests played songs right off the R&B charts. Our repertoire was heavy with tunes by soul music artists: James Brown, Sam 'n Dave, the Wickett Pickett, Jerry Butler, and James and Bobby Purify. Songs on the rhythm and blues music chart had been referred to as "race music," and some black songwriters' songs didn't show profits until bubbly young white singers re-recorded them. For a while, we kids didn't know that Little Richard wrote Pat Boone's *Long Tall Sally* and *Tutti Frutti* or that Big Joe Turner wrote Bill Haley and the Comets' *Shake, Rattle, and Roll*. Nonetheless, we eventually had our musical awakening because in the South, including Gamecock City, we liked our music pure, meaning the black versions of the songs were usually the popular ones with white and black members of the Class of '71. But now, "hard rock" bands were taking over and playing "heavy" music.

Compared to The Tempests and our tight Stax/Volt soul-revue music, this new "heavy" atmosphere at the Teenage Canteen was more like something out of a Cheech and Chong movie. It was all about rock music bands whose musicians sometimes sat (*sat* for Lord's sake! What would James Brown say?) lotus-style on the floor playing Cream and Jethro Tull. And often playing it mighty poorly, may I say. Long-haired, pneumatic girls, probably imported from Shaw Air Force Base, danced around the Teenage Canteen like Grateful Dead groupies, haphazardly waving their hands in the air.

It was a brave new world out there for the Class of '71. The clock was ticking. However, I was far more interested in playing music and getting in good physical shape for football. Was I concerned about this desegregation thing? No. But maybe I should've been.

CHAPTER SEVEN

The Trial Lawyers

A nd so, in the hot summer of 1970, behind the scenes of my summer fun, both villages dissolved. Lincoln High School, with its decades of tradition and well-planned career paths (but no real interaction with the white side of Gamecock City), ceased to exist. Edmunds High School, patrician liberal-arts training center of Gamecock City's ruling class, vanished with its own years of tradition. Verily, a new institution called Gamecock City High School was born. So let it be written, so let it be done, sayeth the Office of Civil Rights.

This all happened in large part due to the work done by the courts and civil rights lawyers such as Thurgood Marshall, Robert Carter, Oliver Hill, Spotswood Robinson, and Jack Greenberg. Russell Brown, Zach Townsend, Willie Smith, Newton Pough, Gamecock City's Ernest Finney, Jr. (later our state's chief justice), and William Bennett pushed the envelope in South Carolina.

But things had *really* started rolling in the late 1940s/early 1950s with Harry and Eliza Briggs suing the school board in

Clarendon County, South Carolina over segregated and unequal education. And man, did they get a raw deal.

Black students in Clarendon County attended Scott's Branch School and the Liberty Hill Colored School (an unpainted wooden shack heated by a fireplace). They were segregated as required by South Carolina law. It's unclear whether black folks in Clarendon County actually wanted desegregation of the schools. At least at first, it appeared that they really just wanted a bus. The bus was important because some of the kids lived nine miles away, and their parents owned no cars.

When black parents asked local school czar R.M. Elliott for a bus, Elliott arbitrarily decided that black people in Summerton weren't entitled to a bus because they didn't pay enough taxes. Certainly, white parents shouldn't be imposed upon to give up one of their 33 buses. And allowing the black and white children to ride the buses together? Ain't gonna happen. The black schoolchildren's parents bought their own bus, but it broke down too often.

After signing a petition regarding the busing matter, Harry and Eliza Briggs lost their jobs, practically before breakfast the next morning. Reverend Joseph Albert DeLaine, a local teacher and minister, and his wife Mattie, signed the petition too. They also lost their jobs. But things were just gettin' started. Reverend DeLaine's church was burned to the ground, and the DeLaines were used for target practice. Both the Briggses and the DeLaines were eventually driven out of town.

Briggs v. Elliott, 98 F. Supp. 529 (E.D.S.C. 1951), was high drama. It was a battle fought by legal eagles. Lead counsel for Superintendent R.M. Elliott and the school board was Bob Figg. Dean of South Carolina's law school and a member of our law firm at the time (but before I was born). Figg was respected by the lawyers on both sides of the case for his sharp mind and courtly ways. The Summerton-area plaintiffs in *Briggs* were represented by Thurgood Marshall, a lawyer for the NAACP's Legal Defense Fund, together with Charleston lawyer Harold R. Boulware.

Thurgood Marshall was a fascinating man. He was born in Baltimore as Thoroughgood Marshall. One day as a young boy he *sua sponte* decided to shorten it to Thurgood. (Can you blame him?) Marshall was about to become a colossus, a mythological god in the pantheon of legal history.

After *Briggs* was reversed by the United States Supreme Court, largely erasing the separate-but-equal doctrine from American jurisprudence, his name was gold. This was not, mind you, the elderly Thurgood Marshall, Supreme Court Justice of the late 1980s and early 1990s who, according to one biographer, allegedly had a drinking problem and who reportedly pursued women (total strangers) on his walks about New York City and Washington, D.C. It was the young, intelligent, and brave lawyer in his prime.

After being sworn in as a Supreme Court Justice in 1967, Marshall was criticized, even by some of his brethren on the high court, for a lack of devotion to the law (e.g., not working hard enough on his opinions and relying too heavily on his clerks). But hey, nobody was criticizing Marshall's devotion to the law in the 1950s and 1960s when he was sleeping in a different bed every night because rednecks were scouring the town trying to throw bombs inside his bedroom. A car of rednecks once veered by Marshall's safe house with a live bomb (what we'd call an IED today). The bomb accidentally exploded. The arm of the man holding the bomb was obliterated. Marshall's protectors ended up having to care for Marshall's would-be assassin. Trial is stressful enough without having to put up with that foolishness.

Marshall had a history of close calls in his younger days. On one occasion, as he and his co-counsel drove away from a Southern courtroom after a day of trial, Marshall's car was pulled over on a county blacktop road by a deputy sheriff. The deputy arrested Marshall, claiming he was driving drunk. With Marshall in the backseat of his police cruiser, the deputy headed down a dirt road to where a group of men awaited with the apparent intent of lynching Marshall. It was only because the other lawyers had followed the patrol car that the deputy eventually actually drove Marshall to the magistrate. The magistrate determined that Marshall was not drunk and set him free.

Marshall was undeniably a hero. Nonetheless, he was a living contradiction: internally inconsistent at times and in some ways a very flawed man. As an associate justice on America's highest court, Marshall made the other Supreme Court Justices uneasy at times. He became frustrated and angry in his later years on the bench when the Warren Court's liberal common law was eroded by newly appointed conservative justices. This manifested itself in the Court's private meetings to discuss how they tentatively planned to vote on the recently heard appeals. Realizing that his viewpoint would be rejected by the conservative majority, he'd break into an Amos and Andy routine: "Yes massa, yes massa," he'd say. Then there was his running feud with extremely liberal Justice William O. "Will Bill" Douglas. Those two birds of a feather did not flock together.

Marshall was, in some ways, as conservative as the white Southerners who hated him so. He was a vehement anti-Communist. This was at a time when Communism and Socialism was perceived as the roadmaps to utopia by many radical left-wing Americans. In Columbia, South Carolina, hippies were waving Red China flags at student protests. Thurgood Marshall had no sympathy for such antics.

You might think that Thurgood Marshall would've been a friend and supporter of Rev. Martin Luther King. Think again. According to one biographer, Marshall resented King and Jesse Jackson and their methods. He believed societal change should be done through the courts and legislatures, not through disorganized street protests. As for black power radicals like the Black Panthers, Marshall was caustic in his comments. He really disliked Louis Farrakhan. Marshall was nearly attacked and beaten by Farrakhan's Fruits of Islam, and he had no love for Malcolm X or the Nation of Islam whatsoever.

When Thurgood Marshall came to Charleston in 1951 to try *Briggs,* the trial was held inside Charleston's Broad Street post office building at the Four Corners of the Law, where the same somewhat moldy, dark-wooded federal courtroom still sits today. *Briggs* would be grouped on appeal with *Brown v. Board of Education of Topeka, Kansas*. Being a Kansas case, the Appellant in *Brown* was supposedly listed first to show that the doctrine was not directed at the South. (Really?) Together, the cases resulted in the end of the separate-but-equal doctrine for the first time in American history.

Briggs was tried before three federal judges, and the appeal went directly to the United States Supreme Court. In some ways, the trial was a charade. The *Briggs* trial was a wrestling match of preconceived notions, collusion, and backstabbing. Before trial, everyone knew or should have known that Judge George Bell Timmerman, Sr. was going to affirm segregation come heck or high water. He was, after all, the Lieutenant Governor's daddy. Conversely, there was no doubt that Judge Julius Waties Waring was going to smack down segregation *in toto*, if he got the chance that is. All eyes were on the swing vote, and the swing vote had a checkered past.

Whether you liked him or not, the guy in the middle was a remarkable man. Judge John Johnson Parker of North Carolina had been an alternate judge at the Nuremburg War Crimes Trials after World War II ended and previously as a special assistant to the Attorney General of the United States in 1923-24. The smart money bet on Parker to vote in favor of upholding desegregation. Supposedly, he actually *fav*ored desegregation but thought it should be done gradually. He'd had his own "issues" with the NAACP relating to alleged racist statements he'd made while running for governor, which ultimately led to him being rejected by the Senate for a seat on the United States Supreme Court.

• • •

Briggs v. Elliott was supposed to be Judge Waties Waring's triumph. His court opinion illuminates the lie in the separate-but-equal doctrine. His words are the wisdom of Solomon itself: "[T]he system of segregation in education adopted and practiced in the State of South Carolina must go and must go now. Segregation is per se inequality." As is usual with Judge Waring, there's good and bad news.

The bad news is that Waring's eloquent words are, well, the dissent. That means that the Briggses, and Judge Waring, lost in a 2-1 vote, with Judge Parker teaming up with Judge Timmerman. The good news is that ultimately Waties Waring's viewpoint was adopted by the United States Supreme Court in *Brown v. Board of Education of Topeka*, 347 U.S. 483 (1954).

Truth is, Waring had long since become an outcast in white Charleston society. A rattlesnake was invited to more parties than the Warings. They were hated by the community at large, and the Warings probably shouldn't have been surprised by it.

For example, Mrs. Waring once gave a speech at the YMCA in Charleston at a time of increasing racial tension. She had leaked to the press the content of her speech in which Mrs. Waring described Southern whites in, let's say, an unflattering light. To be specific, she called Southern whites: "[A] sick, confused and decadent people" who were "introverted, morally weak, and low."

You get the picture. This elicited screams and shouts, as she intended. Why she decided to make this speech is unclear, but unsurprisingly, the meeting didn't end with big hugs between black and white folks, nor did it move the two races a millimeter closer. Judge Waring made sure that the newspaper journalists got printed copies of her speech.

This all ensured that the courageous federal judge who spoke out against the white socio-political establishment of South Carolina would be ostracized, to say the least.

For example, the Warings had a beach cottage on Sullivan's Island. During a coastal thunderstorm, lightning hit a neighbor's beach cottage a few feet away from Judge Waring's house. The neighbor quickly posted a sign reading: "Dear God, he lives next door."

South Carolina's legislature got caught up in the fun. The House of Representatives' Resolution 2177 proclaimed that "necessary funds be allocated to purchase a one-way ticket to any point in the United States of America or preferably a foreign country for Federal Judge J. Waties Waring and his ["socialite wife,"] Mrs. J. Waring Waties[,] provided they leave . . . South Carolina and never again set foot on her soil." Another part of Resolution 2177 suggested that a mule barn at Clemson College be dedicated to the Warings.

Like I said, the Warings didn't get out much. However, the judge did have Thurgood Marshall, the NAACP's lead counsel in the case, over for supper. Now, there's nothing wrong with a judge socializing with lawyers. The judge is, after all, a lawyer whose friends are lawyers too. The odd part of it is that Judge Waring invited Thurgood Marshall over for a meeting *during the litigation itself.* That's not considered improper so long as the other lawyer is invited too. But Bob Figg, the school board's lawyer, was apparently not invited and probably never knew about the dinner date.

It was actually worse. Much worse. While the litigation was pending, Judge Waring specifically advised Thurgood Marshall on how to word his initial brief to the court to ensure that it framed the attack on segregation to Waring's satisfaction. When Marshall's brief wasn't persuasive enough, Judge Waring insisted that Marshall *rewrite* it and told him how to do it. Marshall's brief was submitted to Waring and the other two judges with nothing said about the collusion.

Any first-year law student knows that this, shall we say, "close working relationship" between a judge and one of the parties to a trial, is a disgrace to the legal system. The Code of Conduct for United States Judges wasn't effective until 1973, but to a large extent it merely reflects the proper conduct of judges dating back many years. It provides that:

A Judge Should Avoid Impropriety and the Appearance of Impropriety in All Activities

A. **Respect for Law**. *A judge should respect and comply with the law and should act at all times in a manner that promotes public confidence in the integrity and impartiality of the judiciary.*

B. **Outside Influence**. *A judge should not allow family, social, political, financial, or other relationships to influence judicial conduct or judgment.*

Judicial Code of Conduct Canon 2.

That kind of conduct these days can get a lawyer disbarred and a judge impeached. But it didn't stop there.

After the case went to the Supreme Court, Judge Waring contacted the NAACP and volunteered to help with the appeal of the same case on which he'd been the trial judge. He'd retired from the bench by this time, so despite not being technically illegal, it reeks with the appearance of impropriety and calls into question the integrity of the trial itself. It defeats the purpose of objectivity in judges.

It's not clear why the school board's lawyers didn't move to recuse Judge Waring from the trial anyway. He was, after all, buddies with Walter White, Director of the NAACP, whose lawyers were prosecuting the case. In a final show of bad taste, Waring began maligning Marshall behind his back. Waring complained in letters to Walter White and NAACP board members about Marshall's performance. Waring also suggested that the NAACP hire someone "better" to handle the appeal before the United States Supreme Court. Apparently, Judge Waring believed that you gotta break a few eggs to make an omelet.

Tacky.

There was more meddling by the judiciary. United States Supreme Court Justice Felix Frankfurter was in contact during this period with Philip Elman, Justice Frankfurter's former clerk. Justice Frankfurter attempted to persuade Elman to tailor the

Solicitor General's brief to reflect Frankfurter's opinion that desegregation should happen but happen slowly.[1]

On top of all this, as the *Briggs* trial ended in 1952, the lawyers began packing up their trial materials to leave. One of the lawyers for Clarendon County just *had* to show his behind. He shouted to Marshall, "If you ever show your black ass in Clarendon County again, you'll be dead!"

More tackiness.

These days, the South Carolina Supreme Court requires us to take the Lawyer's Oath which reads thusly: "To opposing parties and their counsel, I pledge fairness, integrity, and civility, not only in court, but also in all written and oral communications."

I guess Clarendon County's counsel accidently took the Redneck's Oath.

---

[1] Sydnor Thompson, *John W. Davis and His Role in the Public School Segregation Cases - A Personal Memoir*, 52 Wash. & Lee L. Rev. 1679, 1686 (1995).

CHAPTER EIGHT

Send in the Kids

There's not much denying that South Carolina's greatest civil rights lawyers graduated from the South Carolina State College, School of Law in Orangeburg. It was created so that there would be an alternative, separate-but-equal law school that would allow blacks to be barred from the University of South Carolina's legal program. South Carolina State Law School was never accredited by the American Bar Association. Suffice it to say that South Carolina's General Assembly was never accused of throwing money at State Law School in its brief existence. Its professors' salaries ranked 45th out of 45 state-supported law schools nationally.

Thurgood Marshall wasn't real impressed with the facilities either. He called State Law School that "Jim Crow dump in South Carolina." But he was wrong. State Law School turned out a brigade of lean, hungry, dedicated lawyers who got the job done, and then some.

Where segregation and housing discrimination were concerned, it usually turned out to be a battle on the one hand between South Carolina State's law school in Orangeburg, with its tiny faculty, and on the other hand, the well-funded University of South Carolina Law School in Columbia. It was a rivalry that puts the Carolina-Clemson games to shame. You might say that civil rights lawyers are the only team from South Carolina State that ever took on South Carolina's two largest universities and beat them like yard dogs.

But of all South Carolina's civil rights attorneys of that era, one man rises above the rest. It was he who, more than anyone else, tore asunder the Gamecock City in which the Class of 1971 had grown up.

A more unlikely candidate for the job could never be found.

Shepard K. ("Shep") Nash, Jr., the school district's influential lawyer and a state senator, didn't care much for Gamecock City's NAACP chapter. In fact, he sued the NAACP in 1956 for defamation. Nash claimed that the Gamecock City branch of the NAACP libeled him by writing that he had pressured people to remove their names from a petition favoring a civil rights issue.

A young NAACP attorney, not well known at the time, Matthew Perry, was dispatched to sort out that case. Nash was a formidable opponent with a sterling reputation. He was President of Gamecock City's Democratic Party, and he'd served in the General Assembly for 14 years. To make things even more dicey for the NAACP, Nash was a president of just about every board and organization worth getting excited about in town. He was Deacon and Trustee at the First Presbyterian Church, as his daddy had been before him. Eventually, Perry recommended that Nash be paid $10,000 in settlement, a small fortune in those days, because of fears that a jury – maybe an all-white one – would hammer the NAACP. But that was just the start of the years-long legal tango Perry and Nash were about to dance.

They went to battle over desegregation of the rural schools in Gamecock County in District Two and urban schools in District 17. The District Two desegregation litigation between Perry and

Nash fell into the lap of newly appointed Judge Robert Hemphill of Chester. The original judge on the case, Timmerman, had gotten tired of running Matthew Perry around the courtroom with a stick, so he retired and handed the stick over to Hemphill, a former WWII bomber pilot and United States Representative. Judge Hemphill didn't care for total desegregation any more than Timmerman, but he didn't want chaos either.

• • •

Clerking for Judge Hemphill was young Ellis Kahn. Now a man with a lot less hair, a bit more profound stomach, and a slower step, Kahn is considered an elder statesman of the Charleston Bar, though he'd surely laugh if you called him that. Back in the mid-1960s, Kahn was a baby law clerk, fresh out of the United States Air Force JAG Corps, who proudly proclaimed to me that in those days he had "zero connection with the South Carolina ruling power structure." Nonetheless, Kahn had a front row seat to the spectacle of just how South Carolina's power brokers reacted when the United States Supreme Court roasted the state on a spit and forced it to desegregate.

The federal and state judiciary in South Carolina were well aware of what happened in the 1962 disaster at Ole Miss in Oxford when the NAACP's lawsuit forced desegregation at the University: it became a riot that turned into a full-blown war. The federal government ended up sending in United States Marshals, the 70th Army Engineer Combat Battalion, the 503rd Military Police Battalion, the Mississippi Army National Guard, and the United States Border Patrol to still the waters. Even then, they couldn't control it. Two people were killed, 160 soldiers were injured, and 28 United States Marshals were hit by gunfire. There'd been nothing like it since Pickett's Charge. Nobody in the judiciary wanted South Carolina to go through what Mississippi had suffered.

Kahn witnessed the district judges and the state supreme court justices, including Chief Justice Moss, talking to one another and working behind the scenes to keep the state calm, even if some of the judges didn't care much for desegregation.

Ellis Kahn vividly remembers one day in particular: Matthew Perry and his protégée Ernest Finney were in the midst of a Gamecock County District Two desegregation hearing. Shep Nash moved into evidence a study showing the supposed inferiority of black people and how they trailed whites by a century. Pretty damning stuff. Ellis Kahn was sitting in Judge Hemphill's courtroom that afternoon as it unfolded. Half a century later, he still evocatively recalls how Matthew Perry slowly rose from counsel table after Nash's argument. Grasping his suit lapels between his thumbs and forefingers, Perry's deep voice filled the courtroom. It "sucked the oxygen out of the room," and with the reverberating hum of Perry's words, the believability of Nash's argument that blacks were intellectually inferior vanished into the mist. The Gamecock County District Two schools were desegregated forthwith.

After the legal artillery was fired, any hope that Lincoln and Gamecock City High Schools would continue to exist as separate black and white schools went down like a buck hit by a Remington. But the battle to totally desegregate Gamecock City's District 17 schools was interwoven with misfortune: political revenge and personal tragedy continued to be front and center.

• • •

The Chief Judge of the Fourth Circuit in January of 1970 was Clement Furman Haynsworth, Jr. He was a true "Old South" legend. (Remember Tuck Haynsworth, the Citadel Cadet from Gamecock County who supposedly fired the first shot of the Civil War? Yes, Clement came from those Gamecock City Haynsworths.) How appropriate that Gamecock City District 17 schools' last great battle in the war to fight immediate total desegregation would land in the lap of a South Carolina judge with roots in Gamecock City.

Judge Haynsworth was the classic Southern Gentleman and the darling of *Time Magazine*. Grey hair combed almost straight back, Haynsworth was said to be a quiet man who loved to raise camellias outside his large Tudor home (described in *Time* as a "$100,000 mansion") in Greenville. Classical music drifted through the rooms and spilled from its windows into the yard. His grandchildren ran in and out, doors slamming. Their laughter splashed from a pool out back. Haynsworth's place was described as elegant but "lived in" (I think that means it needed a paint job). The former Kappa Alpha frat boy never lost his sense of humor or love of practical jokes, even after attending law school at Harvard. He'd done a stint in the Navy during World War II, then was appointed by President Eisenhower to the Fourth Circuit Court of Appeals in 1957. Haynsworth was immediately confirmed by the Senate even though he'd not been a trial judge. Good times were ahead for Judge Haynsworth. Until 1969.

That's when President Richard Nixon nominated Judge Haynsworth to be an associate justice on the Supreme Court. Abe Fortas' bid for the Supreme Court had just suffered a humiliating death in the Senate and was still smoldering in its coffin when Chief Judge Haynsworth was nominated. Resentment by Democrats and liberal Republicans who liked Fortas was palpable in the Senate chamber.

There must've been a long line around the corner of the building filled with disgruntled groups waiting to testify against the Judge. Opponents included the NAACP, the AFL-CIO, and the Leadership Conference on Civil Rights, the latter of which was supposed to be composed of 125 labor, religious, civil rights, and welfare organizations. In the process, Clement Haynsworth was flushed down the toilet. "A sort of laundered segregationist," they called him. "Anti-labor," they claimed. Allegations were made that Haynsworth had failed to recuse himself when a business was before his court in which he had a financial interest. It was ugly. Haynsworth, a quiet man, was borked a decade before borking even became a thing.

The Judge's response to these various allegations was that the groups attacking him were "condemning opinions written when none of us was writing as we are now." When examined as to whether he'd changed over the years, Haynsworth asked rhetorically: "Haven't we all?"

Not good enough, Judge. Hit the road.

By January of 1970, Chief Judge Haynsworth was back at work in Richmond on the Fourth Circuit Court of Appeals, still reeling from his embarrassment in the Senate. He'd been in the papers on and off for three months. Haynsworth had been accused daily of racism, dishonesty, elitism, kicking little baby ducklings – you name it.

So, with nothing left to lose at this point, Judge Haynsworth issued an order in *Stanley v. Darlington County School District* ending the dance for Darlington County once and for all, and in the process, doing the same for his home state of South Carolina:

Whatever the state of progress in a particular school district and whatever the disruption which will be occasioned by the immediate reassignment of teachers and pupils in mid-year, there remains no judicial discretion to postpone immediate implementation of the constitutional principles.

Which means, "the party's over" in English. Judge Haynsworth's order was appealed, but the Supreme Court denied certiorari (refused to hear anything further about a delay in implementing total, immediate desegregation), and that was that. The United States Supreme Court was in no mood to be trifled with.

That spring, some schools had to shut down their separate school systems on a Friday and reopen on Monday with faculties and students completely desegregated. But somehow Gamecock City dodged the bullet and was able to delay the transition until we returned to school a few months later in the fall of 1970.

This fiasco of 1969-1971 is the reason why total desegregation of the schools should never *ever* have been done by the executive or judicial branches. Not that they didn't give it the college try you understand, but neither the courts nor the prosecutors were best suited to tackle this massive change in society. Legislators were the people who should've implemented total desegregation, although there were certainly problems with those folks, too.

Congress and the South Carolina General Assembly could've created committees and commissioned studies into how to properly implement an orderly total desegregation, then set forth clear rules. Legislators could've heard from policy advisors. Public hearings should've been held for opinions and suggestions from the children and their parents who had to endure that upheaval. Public anger might've deflated if the community had gotten better involved.

Instead, what did they do?

Send in the kids.

"And so when they asked for volunteers, we volunteered. Because it had to be done. [H]ad generations prior to us felt that way, then we wouldn't've had to do it. So it had to be done, and we did it," said Theodore Adams, a black student who braved angry faces at Orangeburg High School.

CHAPTER NINE

The Start of Senior Year

The first day of school arrived – August 31, 1970. And so, the federal government informed the Gamecock City School Board of Trustees, "Let the races begin." And thusly, without further ado, the grand experiment was dumped on the Class of '71. The South hadn't seen such a societal-wrenching change in 100 years, since the craziness of Reconstruction.

It was a balmy 78.8 degrees, and you could see for 10 miles. Vietnam was in the midst of its monsoon. Srang in Cambodia was being attacked by North Vietnamese troops, and in the United States, the streets were afire. Police, Black Panthers, and their supporters were at war. The battles ranged from simple fist fighting in Trenton to armed ambuscades of police officers elsewhere. There had been strange sounds coming from a sharecropper shack over in the Concord section of the county, but nobody knew what to make of it. It sounded like the screams of young women and girls. Then again, it was probably just wild animals. (More on this in Chapter 13.)

And down in Gamecock City, the school doors opened, ann-nnnnd…nothing. We just walked in and sat down. No fights, no knifings, no scratching out of the eyes, no violence. School Superintendent McArthur said that it was the quietest and easiest first day of school in years.

The board of trustees believed that it had created a plan designed to make students at both former schools happy. In the short term, sophomores were assigned to Lincoln High School's former campus, and juniors and seniors were moved to the former Edmunds High School campus. Lincoln High and Edmunds High slipped into history, and Gamecock City High School was born from *Brown v. Board of Education.*

• • •

At first, the disagreements were endless. Dixie no longer could be played by the band. In fact, right before our eyes, the word "Dixie" would start to disappear from business' names, children's names, and geographical names. Flying the Confederate flag was verboten. Black power salutes were banned. Many white Gamecock Cityites revolted at the possibility of their children attending *any* school named after Abraham Lincoln, who at the time was still a pariah on the level with General William Tecumseh Sherman. There were so many threats of white flight if 10th graders were required to attend a "Lincoln" campus that the School Board renamed it "Gamecock City High School, 'Council Street' campus." Similar opposition about the "Edmunds" name from black parents ultimately led to the Board renaming the upper school buildings to "Gamecock City High School, 'Haynsworth Street' campus."

In retrospect, it's difficult to believe that the former school administrations were able to come together as they did. You might say that it was like merging the Israeli government and the Taliban in a matter of months, minus the rockets. Gamecock City had to eradicate the segregated black and white school bureaucracies, satisfy internal politics and spheres of influence, and crunch it all together into a single school. I come from a family of educators. Teachers, law professors, and coaches can be, shall we say, contentious and bull-headed on occasion.

Symbolism was as important as the ideas for which they stood. Lincoln High's blue and gold colors became those of Gamecock City High School, and in turn, Edmunds High's gamecock mascot was adopted instead of Lincoln's bulldog.

"Co-people" were created for those student officers elected or appointed. There were co-student council presidents, co-vice presidents, co-King Teens, co-drum majorettes, and co-class beauties. One of the two co-persons was always black and the other was always white. No one questioned this system, and upon reflection, it was flat-out ingenious.

Cub Man was co-student body president together with Larry Blanding, and Nedro was co-senior class president with Albert White. I was a lowly homeroom vice-president. It was ridiculous to even *have* a homeroom vice president. There were no co-people that far down the ladder.

Students from the two former high schools had more in common than we initially knew. Separately but equally, we'd juked and danced to the same music, wore similar clothes, and dreamed of bright futures with great jobs awaiting us. Had the Class of 1971's students paid closer attention to one another, we might've noticed other similarities, too. Some white and black students had the same family names. There were Blandings and McFaddins and Moseses in my classes, which are the names of my relatives.

Some of us probably looked alike, too. If we'd had easy access to DNA tests as we do today, we might've seen even closer ties than a vague resemblance. After all, Gamecock County had been one of South Carolina's larger slaveholding counties in 1860.

The fall of 1970 was an optimistic time for many in the Class of '71. There was hope for the future and hope that the racial problems we were going through would resolve. The Class of '71's mindset was evolving. I recall speculation among classmates looking toward the future, including between one girl (whose name I can't recall) and myself. It happened on the sports field.

"Ya know, this is the first time that 1st graders will start classes with black and white children and then go all the way through to their senior years together," she said.

"Yeah," I said. "When they get to know one another as children, all this fighting will go away."

"I hope so," she replied.

Many of Lincoln High's students were bright, hard-working and would become successful. The same was true for Edmunds High's white and black students. Total desegregation didn't dismiss the case of *Us v. Them,* but it did help.

Many white students at Gamecock City High didn't know just how unequal separate-but-equal education had been, but it became clear to me pretty early in the semester.

It happened in Communism.

Back in those days, Communism was a required course. It was taught using a red textbook that portrayed an unflattering, but accurate portrayal of Soviet Communism. Nobody at Gamecock City High got a diploma, not even a burned one, without passing Communism.

Whether by choice or by chance, the keeper of the key to passing this half-credit course devolved upon Miss Margaret Dunning. Born in 1912, she was about 59 years old in 1971, but Miss Dunning had allowed herself to age prematurely in Gamecock City. Her white hair was still coiffed true to the fashion of the 1930s when she'd been a schoolgirl at the College of Charleston. Her conservative dress really contrasted with the short skirts of the younger teachers. I never saw Miss Dunning smile or crack a joke. Ever. Then again, our conversations were limited solely to me answering, "Here" when she called the attendance roll.

The truth is that she was an interesting lady who, according to co-teacher J. Grady Locklear, enjoyed a flute of wine as much as anyone. But she was from a different era. Miss Dunning was used to the old Edmunds High School way of doing things. At

Edmunds High, class discipline hadn't been such a great problem. Discipline had been enforced quickly and effectively, but times had changed.

Miss Dunning had difficulty controlling black students in Communism class from day one. She seemed confused and quite frustrated by it. She was a concerned teacher, worried that after 12 years of going to school, students in her class wouldn't graduate because they failed her half-credit course.

One day in Communism, after handing back a graded, make-it-or-break-it test, Miss Dunning asked everyone who had failed the test to walk into the hallway for a meeting. Miss Dunning wanted to tell them in private that she was going to set up remedial classes so that they might bring up their class grades and graduate on time. Every former Lincoln student rose and walked into the hall with her. Every white student stayed seated. So much for the sophism "separate-but-equal."

• • •

A particularly notable English teacher was Mrs. Carolyn McKay. She taught Advanced Senior English our final year and really knew her stuff. She was the first black teacher that most of the white students in that classroom had ever had. Mrs. McKay was a very tall lady, well over six feet high, and was a true professional from her class preparedness and demeanor right down to her dress. She had a master's degree from South Carolina State College. Apropos to her sweet, in-class demeanor, she was advisor to the Bible Club.

Mrs. McKay had no trouble controlling her mostly white Senior English class. None of the boys or girls in our class, even Ms. Soon-To-Be Attack Divorce Trial Attorney Beverly K. Ballinger, gave her any lip.

Carolyn McKay made school interesting. She was quick with a laugh when amused, and thinking back on it, she was often amused, especially when it came to the boys in our class. Mrs. McKay was the type of teacher who always had a smile for us as we walked in her room. And on this notable day, she did just that. Mrs. McKay greeted us at the door with a smile, and we all settled down after a while and started talking about some aspect of literature. It was midday, around lunch time. Suddenly, there was a slam on the door as if someone had slapped it with the palm of his or her hand. The slam was accompanied by some loud, pseudo-angry voices for 30 seconds or so before the noise dissipated. No one entered the room.

It was "the riots."

For most of us, it seemed like the riots came out of the blue. Maybe some black and white kids gave one another the fisheye in the halls, but overall, Gamecock City High School was a large school and these sorts of things seemed to vanish into thin air pretty quickly. There were relatively minor incidents now and then. According to Superintendent McArthur, on one occasion, a white Golden Gloves champ attacked a black student who responded with a weapon. Both were kicked out of school. After investigating the incident, only the black student was readmitted.

The transition appeared to be going pretty smoothly from the administrators' points of view, but there was still an underlying tension. Rumors abounded. For example, the incident between the Golden Gloves champ and the black student was described in the rumor mill as having been adjudicated by expulsion of the black student (only). There was another rumor that a nosy neighbor had seen a white student get kissed on the school's front steps by a black student. The neighbor called the police who supposedly arrested the couple. Allegedly, the administration wasn't aware of this rumor mill.

Yet, these misapprehensions didn't only exist between students. Some members of the faculty were just as guilty. A white coach once told Superintendent McArthur that black players were "unreliable." Supposedly, they'd just give up if the team got behind in a game. A black coach told the superintendent that white players simply can't play basketball – period. There was agreement among some of the men and women teachers that white female teachers would have trouble handling black students.

These implicit biases of the faculty seeped into the curriculum. In her history class, Emma Harvin, a black student at Gamecock City High School who loved history, got a dose of, shall we say, "alternative genetics." It was taught as part of her South Carolina history course. The class began studying evolution. The teacher said that the black "nation of people came from monkeys and apes."

Jobs as department directors and head-coaching jobs were plums. Everyone wanted them when the schools combined. The important administrative positions (principal, vice principal, etc.) and department chair positions typically were awarded to white teachers. For example, the Board appointed Bobby Matthews as principal of the flagship campus (the upper school comprising the 11th and 12th grades). Matthews, who was white, was a former head football coach and an experienced administrator. However, Coach Matthews had never been principal at either of the two high schools. Meanwhile, United States Air Force veteran Earl Vaughn had already been the principal at Lincoln High for six years. Vaughn was kept on his old campus as principal of the 10th grade students while Coach Matthews took the more prestigious upper-school principal position.

Like many, if not most, places across the South, Gamecock City is a football town, so being appointed to a "coachship" is truly prized. The locals, by and large, didn't care much about who got hired as Chair of the Psychology Department. To them, the high-profile head football coaching job was more important than any other administrative or departmental position. "Coach" is more a title of nobility than a job designation in the South.

I once defended a case in Berkeley County where the plaintiff was a coach who'd allegedly been injured in a wreck with my client. The coach looked really healthy to me, but his case was otherwise strong. The coach's lawyer, a transplant from up North, kept working on me to pay more money:

"You need to settle this case," he said at a mediation conference. "The jury's gonna love him."

"Yeah, and why is that?" I asked.

"Well, he's a coach, isn't he?" the plaintiff's attorney asked.

"He is," I replied.

"Well, most *all* coaches are royalty down here in the South."

Thinking about it, we did end up paying the coach quite
well.

• • •

The head football coaching position for the 1970-71 academic
year went to Steve Satterfield, the charismatic former University
of South Carolina's star quarterback. Tall, handsome, male-model
thin, and confident, he was precious to Gamecock City. The
prior year, Satterfield had a magical record. He'd won the state
championship in South Carolina's largest school division with
the best win-loss record in South Carolina history. Coach knew
how to build a "team," such that 40 years later at our high school
reunion, the football players in the room still gravitated to one
another in small groups as friends. That's what team building is
all about, and that was Satterfield's specialty. Athletes who play
together and feel themselves part of a brotherhood or sisterhood
will, all things even, triumph over a collection of highly-talented,
maverick players. Satterfield also had compiled a coaching staff
of extraordinary assistants and built a well-organized feeder program at the junior high and junior varsity levels.

One of these assistant coaches was Jack Williams, who had
been head coach at Lincoln High for one year before total desegregation interrupted his career plans. Coach Williams never
complained about his new position (that I knew of, at least).
Still, despite Edmunds High's first-rate team, it must've been
tough to drop down a notch.

Freddie Solomon, a rising senior and member of the Class
of '71, was a similar case in point. He allegedly had been an
underutilized, second-string quarterback at Lincoln High under

Williams during his junior year. Once the Gamecock City High School football coaches got a look at Freddie in spring practice, he was immediately moved up to first team quarterback.

Maybe Freddie wasn't quite ready at Lincoln High. Maybe Coach Williams wasn't ready for Freddie. Maybe it was merely an unfounded rumor. Who knows? But under Satterfield, he became a star. Freddie went on to play college football and eventually turned pro. He played for the San Francisco 49ers, catching a touchdown pass from Joe Montana in the Super Bowl and mentoring stars like Jerry Rice. He led the Gamecock City High football team to otherworldly success that year that ultimately ended in a loss in the state semi-finals to the eventual 4-AAAA champs. But, after the stellar season ended, a crisis erupted.

That crisis was that Head Coach Steve Satterfield got an offer to coach on the college level and immediately gave his notice to Gamecock City High School. Gamecock City High's administration now had to choose between two of Satterfield's assistant coaches: Bill Noonan and Jack Williams. Coach Noonan was as smart as a whip, quite experienced, and thus very qualified. He inspired loyalty in his players and was recommended for the head coach position by Steve Satterfield himself. He'd been an integral part of the 4-AAAA championship team and the wonderful 1969 season.

Yet, Williams was qualified too. He'd already been a head coach, unlike Bill Noonan. The year before, when he hadn't gotten the head coaching job, Williams had been a team player about it and had not thrown a hissy fit. Nonetheless, fate was not in favor of Coach Williams. Noonan got the chateaubriand; Williams got the pig foot.

Grumbling began to surface when word escaped that Lincoln's former head coach was passed over for the second time. Lord knows Williams was not amused. He told the school administration point blank, "You made a bad decision. You did not choose the most qualified man."

And that was just the start. Reportedly, Coach Williams showed up at the basketball game against Manning High School in the holiday tournament and, with a clenched fist, raised his arm before the crowd in a black power salute. That might've been a rumor, or it might've been the truth, but one thing was sure: suddenly, every black male Gamecock City High basketball player had found something he'd forgotten to do and didn't show up for the next game.

Gamecock City High's basketball team instantly found itself lily-white right before a tournament. The black and white cheerleaders stayed and cheered for the entire tournament.

Innocently sucked into faculty politics, the black players, some of whom were surely college prospects, got kicked off the team and lost that all-important senior year of basketball forever. Coach Williams walked out of Gamecock City High School at the end of the spring semester. He didn't ask for a job recommendation. School Superintendent Laurin McArthur, Jr. in his book years later made it pretty clear that Williams didn't have a prayer of a chance of getting one anyway.

Nonetheless, life bumped along in Gamecock City. Like weeds clawing their way to flower through cracks in cement, young love sprouted at Gamecock City High School amidst the desegregation disruptions. For me, it began in Algebra II. I sat next to a 16-year-old girl I'd never seen or heard of before that year. She was a natural beauty, a tiny-waisted princess with long, black, wavy hair like a lioness's mane. And I fell in love.

Sumter High School: Haynsworth Street Campus (Grades 11-12).

PHOTO CREDIT: The Paragon

Lincoln High School, circa 1935-1950: An old insurance photo of
the front of Lincoln High School. There were additional buildings
in use by the time total desegregation occurred but which are
not shown. Notice that like the "white school," Lincoln High's
classroom windows were open, owing to a lack of air conditioning.

PHOTO CREDIT: From the collection at the South Carolina
Department of Archives and History (S 112113 No. 2335).

C.A. Wilson was a star athlete and running back of the year
in South Carolina's largest football division as a junior. He
attended Alice Drive Junior High School as part of President
Nixon's Freedom of Choice plan. His reception was chilly
at first, at least until he was accepted as the star athlete that
he was and his genial personality had become manifest.

PHOTO CREDIT: The Paragon

Ned Parker: Co-President of Gamecock City's Class of '71, he
attended a Ku Klux Klan rally in the parking lot of a local racetrack.
At the rally, Parker drew a crowd as he argued out loud with the
Klansmen, telling them that they were wrong in their beliefs and
that he liked the black students at our school "more than you." He
was not well-received and came close to dying for his beliefs.

PHOTO CREDIT: The Paragon

Klansmen preparing to deliver a speech before the faithful.

PHOTO CREDIT: Sloan, Eugene B. Photograph of
KKK rally near Rantowles, S.C., 29 July 1967. Kathleen
Lewis Sloan and Eugene B. Sloan Collection, South
Caroliniana Library, University of South Carolina

Class of '71 Varsity Basketball Team: After yet another controversy
arose, this time over which assistant coach should be chosen
as head football coach for the upcoming school year, black
basketball players at Gamecock City High School were absent
from future basketball games. The basketball team quickly found
itself lily white but still managed to have a winning season.

PHOTO CREDIT: The Paragon

Class of 1971 Varsity Football Team: As often the case across
the South, athletes served as a bastion of stability amidst racial
unrest. Black and white athletes at Gamecock City High
School were no different. Many of them had been playing
sports together for four years before reaching their senior years.
The Gamecock City High football players had enjoyed an
undefeated junior varsity year and an undefeated varsity season
before total desegregation took place their senior year.

PHOTO CREDIT: The Paragon

Essex Durant: Offensive guard on the Class of '71's varsity football team, all around "character," and known (mainly by himself) as Essex the "Sex Machine," he was, like Leon Pack, a stabilizing factor amidst the turmoil surrounding the Class of '71. Durant saw neither race nor color and sought to be included in no cliques, except sports teams.

PHOTO CREDIT: The Paragon

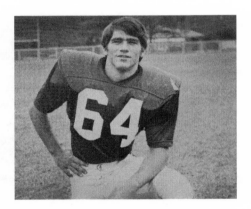

Feisty Curtis Hammock: After a disagreement in study hall between Hammock and a black student, they readdressed the disagreement in the cafeteria foyer, but it was over between the two students quickly. However, the news spread amongst the student bodies at the two campuses, culminating into what some described as a "riot." At football practice that afternoon, things were as calm as always though.

PHOTO CREDIT: The Paragon

Darcelle Henry-Mack, Nancy Howle Patterson and the inimitable Leighton Cubbage: The times were a-changing, as was fashion. The togs and hairstyles of Darcelle Henry-Mack (standing), Nancy Howle Patterson (gazing upon flowers), and the Ferguson twins (pictured on page 85), were indicative of this.

PHOTO CREDITS: Nancy Howle Patterson and The Paragon

Leighton Cubbage: The inimitable Leighton Cubbage.

PHOTO CREDIT: The Paragon

School Superintendent Laurin McArthur (top): A former naval officer in the Battle of Leyte Gulf, Dr. McArthur nonetheless found himself sailing unfamiliar waters when the Class of '71 threw together different cultures on short notice.

Former football coach, administrator, and Korean War Veteran Bobby Matthews, (below, left), was Principal of the upper school (11th and 12th grades).

Dr. J. Earl Vaughn, (below, right), was Principal of the lower school (10th grade) at the Council Street Campus. He, like Bobby Matthews, was well respected in Gamecock City for, *inter alia*, his community service and having served in the United States Air Force for several years. Education runs in the family: His son, Gregory J. Vaughn of Atlanta, received his medical degree at Harvard Medical School and wrote his thesis on the Class of '71.

PHOTO CREDIT: The Paragon

Mrs. Carolyn T. McKay: A gentle, scholarly, and conservative woman, she was the first black teacher for many white students. Mrs. McKay taught English Literature, and she made it interesting.

PHOTO CREDIT: The Paragon

The Ferguson twins: For some reason, despite their somewhat-reduced stature, it was hard to miss Yulaundra and Fernaundra, a.k.a., the Ferguson twins. Their father was a retired Master Sergeant in the United States Air Force, and the twins were politically active that 1970-71 year. When traveling across country, their parents made sure that there was a military installation nearby at the end of the day so that the family could sleep there without being turned away.

PHOTO CREDIT: The Paragon

The Soiling of Old Glory is a photograph taken by Stanley Forman during the Boston busing crisis on April 5, 1976. The white man, Joseph Rakes, is seen assaulting black lawyer Ted Landsmark with a flagpole affixed with the American flag. Forman caught the moment and won a Pulitzer Prize, one of his three such awards for the photograph the following year. The irony of a black man being attacked with an American flag in Boston while Gamecock City in South Carolina was relatively quiescent, is not hard to miss.

PHOTO CREDIT: Stanley Forman

Site of the 1970 Ku Klux Klan Rally - Gamecock Speedway's parking lot, as it looks today.

PHOTO CREDIT: Warren Moise

Chief Judge Haynsworth: Chief Judge Clement Furman
Haynsworth, Jr.'s family had roots in Gamecock City. When
nominated as Chief Judge of the Fourth Circuit Court of Appeals, he
was confirmed by the Senate with relatively little acrimony. However,
the political landscape had changed radically when he was nominated
by President Nixon for the United States Supreme Court. Things
turned quite ugly. After losing his bid to become an Associate Justice,
he drove back to Richmond. Thereafter, when South Carolina school
districts appealed for delays in federal courts, including those by
Gamecock City, Judge Haynsworth followed the letter of the law.

CREDIT: Moore, Van, photographer. Photograph of Clement
Furman Haynsworth, Jr., Photograph. Van Moore Studio:
Greenville, c 1950-1959. Photographs Haynsworth, South
Caroliniana Library, University of South Carolina. The writing
on the photo appears to be "To my old friend, Fritz Hollings."

CHAPTER TEN

Peace, Love, Music, and Hot Pants

Love sprouts through the most corrupt soil, from the most polluted waters, and under the most cataclysmic circumstances. My belle's name was, well, let's call her Ellie McKissick. Miss McKissick wore cloth belts in her blue jeans and turquoise rings, which was the style of the day. But she looked her best while sporting a blessing from the fashion industry – "hot pants." Hot pants were called "short shorts" in the 1950s and had made a comeback.

Miss McKissick was quick witted and sharp as a tack. She studied a good bit and made better grades than I did, but that was a fairly low threshold to beat anyway. Unlike my parents, who had adopted a laissez-faire attitude (at best) regarding my choice of a college, she and her mom were driving to universities around the southeast, looking for the best school for her chosen career. No one in my family ever did anything like that. Besides, like my other siblings, I was going to go to the University of South Carolina. No need to drive around the country.

Over the course of my senior year, I had gotten to know Ellie pretty well. At least as well as any immature and insecure 17-year-old boy can understand a pleasant, pretty, young woman. I was crippled by an irrational fear of her rejection that rose to the level of a psychosis. However, I did know that if she had a headache, I wanted to be her aspirin.

Lightning first struck in Mr. Schroer's Algebra II class.

Miss McKissick and her friend Janice McDaniel sat next to me. She wore a culotte skirt and a navy-blue blouse buttoned at the top. Miss McKissick's countenance had the breathtaking simplicity of a fair young maiden gazing unconcernedly into the distance from a Rembrandt canvas.

Staring at her pulchritude across the aisle in Algebra II was the idyllic state of affairs in my adolescent life when the "riots" really heated up. Although the "riots" lasted only one day, they reoccurred in spatterings during the rest of the week. Some after-shocks were worse than others. For this one, students began to trickle into the halls in response to the chaos. I became inspired by Southern chivalry. Sensing the notion that good manners might pay dividends, I leaned across the aisle to Miss McKissick and asked:

"Are you plannin' to stay the rest of the day? I mean, are you goin' home early and all?"

We could hear turmoil outside in the halls, so I felt my question was not unreasonable. Nonetheless, my face flushed with the fear of rejection. After all, Miss McKissick was dating a college freshman despite the fact that she was only a high-school junior. She'd probably never be interested in me.

"I think I'm goin' home now," she said, not a bit frightened by the commotion.

"I'll walk you to your car. Let's go," I replied.

"Mr. Schroer, we're goin' home. No disrespect, sir," I informed the teacher, being a man about it and all.

So, Ellie McKissick and I slipped out. We walked down the old wooden hall to the back door. There were no students out in the parking lot, agitated or otherwise. Ellie drove an old sports car. Notebook paper, composition books, and balled-up napkins were in disarray on the seats and floorboard. As she slid into the bucket seat, she crooked her finger motioning me toward her open window. I leaned over, and Miss McKissick gave me a peck on the cheek.

"Thanks for looking after me. I 'preciate it," she said. "May I ask you something?"

"It's nothin'," I replied. "Of course you can ask me a question. Shoot."

"Well, would you like to come to the LCC dance with me next month?" she asked.

"LCC" was short for *Les Coeurs Cogniae*. Roughly translated from French into English, it was supposed to mean "The Heartbreakers." LCC was an invitation-only high school social club composed of junior and senior high school girls from Gamecock City High School and the private schools throughout the county. LCC was Gamecock City's equivalent of a Delta Delta Delta Sorority. Anyway, I had no special plans for "next month" (the entire month), and I was quite willing to attend the party. So, I said, "I'd love to go," and immediately my insecurity began pulling at the ribbons of her gift. Was her college friend unable to attend? Does she feel sorry for me? Was she regretting it already?

• • •

A few weeks later, on the Saturday morning of the LCC Dance, I picked up a corsage for Miss McKissick at a local florist. I shampooed my hair several times and used Suave conditioner to make it smell good. No need to shave... Then, as night fell,

I drove to her house, a ranch style home across town on a lake called Second Mill. It was a big date for me.

Young women just don't understand how they're seen by young boys. In my mind, girls just seemed so sure of themselves and so poised. I, on the other hand, was often ill at ease, quick to imagine a slight, and perceived myself as a social bumbler. Of course, at that age, boys (especially me), have much to feel inferior about.

I knocked on the door.

"How do you do?" her mother asked, opening the door. Mrs. McKissick was a pleasant woman dressed casually but fashionably, with short brown hair with blonde highlights.

Ellie glided into the living room with the natural grace of a countess receiving a yard man. I can still see that glimmering white-toothed smile in my mind a half-century later. She wore a white blouse with dark, crushed-velvet pants. I was stylishly bedecked in dressy elephant-bell blue jeans and a loose silk shirt with balloon sleeves.

Her father, a Lieutenant Colonel in the United States Air Force, came in to say hello. He was tall and spare of frame with closely cropped hair, almost a flat top. In retrospect, Lieutenant Colonel McKissick treated me more courteously than I ever treated my own daughter's beaus, but daddies made me nervous, so I got Ellie out of there quickly.

It was a cool evening as Ellie and I walked beneath the pine trees covering her lawn to my mother's Ford station wagon parked in the driveway. I'd worried for several days about how to keep the conversation going as we drove. The LCC party was in a cheaply constructed clubhouse at Poinsett State Park. When things got quiet, I managed to fill the dead air with my historical knowledge. The park was named for Joel Poinsett. The Poinsettia plant, found on every doorstep during the Christmas season, is attributed to him.

"The Poinsetta flower isn't really a flower," I observed. "It's actually a brilliant red leaf."

She didn't know that.

Chaperones were inside when we arrived, mothers of LCC members. A banquet table covered with a white vinyl tablecloth was on one side of the room. On top were some of the cheapest refreshments I'd seen in a while, including unbearably sweet cherry Kool-Aid, regular potato chips, and an orange charlotte for dessert. All was quite proper. LCC parties inspired full and complete attendance by the local socialites. The joint was packed.

Being an Air Force kid, Miss McKissick had lived in more of the world than had I. She had absolutely nothing to fear from me. I was virtuous to a point of distraction, and our relationship remained more platonic than I'd like, straight through to the bitter end. Regardless, I was deeply in love with her, drunk on that volatile teenage cocktail of unreasoning jealousy and heavenly euphoria that makes young lives a rollercoaster ride. Love at the age of 17 is so intense that it's painful. There should be a psychological diagnosis for it. Once pharmaceutical companies figure out how to make money from "youth," it'll be given a diagnostic code and a pseudo-medical name in the Diagnostic and Statistical Manual of Mental Disorders. They'll call it something like Adolescent Infatuation Syndrome, come up with an acronym (e.g., "AIS") to market it, and create a drug that does absolutely nothing for a syndrome that does not exist. Sorta like fibromyalgia. Anyway, by the end of the evening, I'd worked up the courage to give Ellie a kiss outside by the lake, and we were off on a ride that would last the rest of my senior year.

• • •

In between dates with Miss McKissick, I played with a band from the tiny town of Dalzell near Stateburg. Today, I think we'd be called a country-pop group. However, we'd play just about any song in the record books, so long as somebody knew the words to at least one verse and chorus.

The other musicians in the group were at least thirteen years older than I. Now that I'm 67 years old, a thirteen-year age gap isn't significant. However, when thirteen years lie between an immature high schooler and a grown man of 30 with twins, a wife, and a mortgage, well, it's quite a different matter. And that was just the case. Jimmy, the guitarist, Al, our bass player, and Donnie all had children of their own, not much younger than I. They were men. I was a boy.

We played some bars and parties, nothing very big. But one gig sticks out among the rest. It was in a small nightclub that crouched like a toad beside the Forest Acres entrance to Fort Jackson. Our band was scheduled to play there one evening. The nightclub was constructed of painted cinderblocks. A red neon Budweiser sign hung in the white-curtained windows on the parking lot. Welded in place in front of the emerald front door was an iron-grated protective cage to discourage burglars. Earlier that day, I'd driven to Dalzell after school let out, and there, I hopped into Jimmy's car with the other guys. We rode down Highway 378, talking the drive away, our musical equipment trailer bouncing behind us. The band got to Columbia at about 6 p.m. and quickly unloaded the trailer. We humped the equipment to the back of the nightclub and set it up next to the pool table.

The nightclub's decor was like hundreds of other places I'd play over the years. Filthy brown industrial carpet – thin as a piece of paper – covered a concrete-slab floor. Throughout the seating area were square, wood-veneer tabletops, each supported by a single chrome pedestal with four black iron legs sprouting from the bottom. Ceramic ashtrays decorated with Michelob logos were on all tables. In those days before grocery stores carried multiple specialty beers, Michelob was as good as it got in South Carolina. Offering Michelob for sale gave the bar a patina of respectability and proved the nightclub owner to be a man or woman of style and taste.

Like some of the customers' missing teeth and sideways-leaning noses, the furniture was battle weary. Cigarette burns scarred the tables and chairs alike. Years had passed since the nightclub had celebrated a full house. The owner must've been going broke just keeping the doors open.

That evening I played a little white Farfisa Fast Five Combo Organ. After the first set, the air was stale and dead. The place was mostly empty, peppered with locals, all over the age of 40, some G.I.s, and a couple of older women in beehives. We were playing *For the Good Times* by Ray Price when the excitement happened. A difference of opinion broke out beside the pool table on my immediate left.

Bars, especially low-rent bars where I've since spent a lot of time as a musician, have certain rules of civil procedure. Rule #1 is never put your quarter on the pool table where the most obnoxious drunk – the one looking to fight – is playing a game. Rule #2 requires everyone to be nice to the bouncer and laugh at his jokes. Rule #3 is that if you hit on the bar owner's girlfriend, you do so at your own risk; this could lead to all sorts of problems, including the bouncer ejecting your skinny behind into the parking lot.

This particular night, there was a violation of Rule #1. A GI made the mistake of putting his quarter beside a local loudmouth's quarter on the pool table. I saw a quick blur then realized the loudmouth had broken a pool stick across the transgressor's skull. I'd never seen that before or since. Already unconscious, if not dead or brain-damaged, the victim went down like a sack of flour. The next thing we knew, it was as if someone had stomped on a fire ant mound. GIs were leaping about everywhere – lunging, falling, kicking, and punching.

The mob advanced toward the band. I picked up my organ and while still watching the brawl to my left, I took a step toward the right. In doing so, I bumped against Jimmy, who was holding his red Hagstrom solid-body guitar by the neck with both hands like a baseball bat. The rest of the guitar was behind his back. Jimmy was going to brain somebody with that Hagstrom, if need be.

The fight escalated and moved into the parking lot. We were still by our musical equipment. There was a gunshot. The manager, a short, balding man who looked like Rat Pack comedian Joey Bishop, had shot someone with a revolver right outside the front door. We quickly packed up and hit the road back to Gamecock County lest we be seen as witnesses. After that, I decided that maybe I'd take a short break from the music business. Oh well, more time for Ellie.

One morning, at the end of the year, I received a telephone call from Miss McKissick. Seniors were already out of school, but the underclassmen had to continue for several days. Miss McKissick had picked up my yearbook for me and signed it. She asked that I come by so she could give it to me. Later that day, I arrived at her home. She met me at the front door with a sweet smile. After some small talk, Miss McKissick broke my pitiful little heart. We were "going our separate ways," was all I can recall her saying. After that, the Earth pretty much stopped turning. I put up no fight. After all, what can you really do in that situation but try and retain your dignity by leaving? When I got home, I read the Gamecock City High School yearbook. I saw she'd written a Dear John note inside.

I pined for Miss McKissick terribly that summer of 1971. I was unyielding in my refusal to contact her. I was, after all, a *real* man. So, we both spent her final summer in Gamecock City driving the same streets, going to the identical parties, and shooting glances at one another across rooms, but never speaking. When Miss McKissick called to see me just once more before she moved away, I had purposely left town, taking a trip to Garden City Beach. What ironclad resolve I had back then. What a fool.

At Christmas, she returned to Gamecock City for a visit, called me, and asked me to come see her, which I did. She invited me to visit her in her new home, and I declined, but for a long time, there was never a day when she didn't cross my mind for at least a few seconds, just enough to arrest my thoughts and bring her pretty 17-year-old face to mind.

Many years later, I was in Atlanta doing research on a historical book. I ran into Alan Charpentier, an old friend from Gamecock City, at the Hyatt where I stayed. That evening we met for supper and began to shoot the breeze about members of our high school class. Alan was divorced, claimed he was happy as could be, and was in Atlanta for a swimming pool sales convention. I was separated from my wife but remained chaste and faithful. We retired to the piano bar where I lit up a Swisher Sweet cigar.

"You know she's here, don't you?" he said.

We were listening to the pianist, a jazz afficionado whose left hand was as controlled and facile as his right hand.

"Who is 'she'?" I asked.

"Ellie McKissick. She's divorced and lives in a townhouse off the beltway. Why don't you give her a call? She'd love to see you, I'll bet."

I thought about that.

"Alan," I said. "You know, some things are best left as memories." And we just ended it with that.

CHAPTER ELEVEN

The Athletes

Young love was one flower sprouting amongst the weeds; the other was the football team on which I was a 149-pound tight end. The football team was a relative oasis of peace that fall of 1970. After all, at junior-high and high schools, white kids had been playing sports with black kids since the mid-1960s. These racially integrated sports teams in the mid-1960s had become part of the schools' fabric, and the black players were well liked. Football players from Lincoln High School had been surreptitiously practicing with us since late spring of 1970. The only students from the segregated Lincoln High and Edmunds High that had spent a significant amount of time together before classes began in September were from the football team, give or take a limited number of meetings between student body leaders.

Up in South Boston during its desegregation disaster, football was completely abolished for the entire year. Thankfully, that wasn't the case for us. In Gamecock City, black and white members of most sports teams remained friends, despite the suspicion and resentment within the regular student body. We would go to classes, meetings, rap sessions, and the like during the day. Then, at 3:30 p.m., everyone showed up on the football field. It was a thing of great beauty, or maybe it was just another example of the case of *Us v. Them*, "us" being the football team and "them" being the rest of the school.

At Gamecock City High School, black and white teammates were bound together at all hours of the day: before or after practice, it didn't matter. We were friends. I often gave some of my teammates of color rides home. I shouldn't say "home," because I never really saw their houses. As we got near their neighborhoods, invariably I'd hear, "Drop me off at the store," or "I'll get off at the corner."

"No man," I'd say, "I'll drop you off at your house."

Eventually I understood – some of them were embarrassed about where they lived. Thereafter, I didn't press the issue. They got dropped off at the store.

As Dr. Earl Vaughn put it, "[This] program...not only brought our staff and students together, [but also] brought our community together."

On Friday afternoons during the football season, there wasn't much time between the final bell at 3:10 p.m. and 5:00 p.m. when we had to be back on campus for the pre-game supper at Big Jim's Restaurant. Many of us just stayed at school and hung around together. Our bonds weren't limited to the practice field. The football teams (varsity and non-varsity) got along well, shuckin' and jivin' in the hallways in between regular classes too.

But this comradery wasn't always easily swallowed by other members of the community. One Friday, my father told me before I left school that if I didn't get a haircut, I couldn't come home that night. Three of my teammates, Curtis Hammock, Essex Durant, Leon Pack, and I went to a barbershop near Lawson's Drugstore in a little strip plaza. The barber was a thin man in his 20s or 30s with dark, straight hair and a chipped front tooth. He was also a football afficionado who followed Gamecock High School football religiously and knew our weekly team stats.

I'd been in the barbershop a few times, and we'd always had a cordial relationship. As I sat in his barber chair on this Friday, Curtis, Essex, and Leon took seats in the waiting area. The barber was acting strangely. In lieu of his customer-friendly smile, his expression was flat.

"They can't come heeyuh," the barber said.

The strip plaza was a student hangout near Alice Drive Junior High School. I supposed he must've had one of those rules whereby only one or two students at a time could enter.

"What you mean?" I asked innocently.

"*They* can't come in here," he said, pointing to Essex and Leon, who were black.

I was still trying to put this together when Essex stood up.

Then it hit me. He won't let our buddies enter the barber shop because they were black. That pissed me off, and I imagined how humiliated Essex and Leon must've been.

"We just wait outside," he said.

"No man," I said. "I'm coming too."

We left that dump and never went back.

It wasn't only local community members that couldn't wrap their heads around our interracial friendships. Even my dad gave some initial pause to the fellowship. My father had a tradition of grilling hamburgers after Gamecock City High School football games. One evening that fall, I showed up to supper with Essex behind me.

Essex (pronounced "Essie") Durant played offensive guard on the football team. Throughout his life, he enjoyed several nicknames. As a child, he was called "Boobie."

However, when he was around the Class of '71, Essex preferred to refer to himself as "Essex, the Sex Machine." He was hilarious, with an off-the-wall sense of humor. Essex had a practice of making up words out of nowhere, like "scruh-*scrunh*-scruh," which meant absolutely nothing. Essex ignored cliques. You might say that his sports buddies were the closest Essex came to a clique. This included the baseball team where he played catcher and also the football team. Lord knows, Essex Durant had no political aspirations.

I'll never forget that initial tension when I first brought Essex to that home barbeque. I had never brought a black friend home for supper or otherwise. Gamecock City's blacks and whites had never mixed socially in any meaningful numbers. After a couple of minutes of unsurety, my family took to him like a duck to water. Daddy threw another hamburger on the grill, and we jumped in. Essex ended up making guest appearances at my brothers' annual family campouts for years.

So, sports, in their own odd way, served as a sort of glue for desegregation. The friendships we developed on our team transcended color. They were instilled early, and they felt natural. We had overcome challenges together, celebrated successes together, and mourned losses together. We were friends, and ultimately always had each other's backs. When we weren't going to war together on the field, we were going through war together in our community.

• • •

I was with my football buddies when the first battle erupted in our school. That day, the cafeteria was jammed with chattering students. Around the walls were professional aides: big, burly men in dark slacks, short-sleeved white polyester dress shirts, and clip-on neckties. They were the school board's bouncers. They tiptoed about, quiet as humongous tabby cats. Rectangular white-topped folding tables surrounded by grey metal chairs were jammed in lines across the cafeteria from front to back. I sat at the first table in the front with my teammates. Although it was first period study hall, we were doing anything and everything but studying. Herbert Baker, a quiet white boy and halfback on the football team, patiently ate a cinnamon roll. Unlike most football players, Baker was shy and never complained, even at practices in the debilitating South Carolina summer heat.

At the table beside us, a skinny black guy threw a sharp-edged, stainless-steel napkin holder at another student who was seated across his table. It missed and flew to our table, hitting Herbert. Throwing a steel napkin holder with sharp, pointed edges is an idiotic gesture (it was reported in the *New York Times* as involving an empty milk carton playfully thrown by a girl at another black student). The black guy probably meant no harm to his friend and surely didn't intend to hurt Herbert. Curtis Hammock, a 150-pound offensive guard on the football team, was sitting beside Herbert. Curtis was small but entirely fearless. He overreacted and posed a rhetorical question of sorts:

"Why doh you look where you frowin' nat thing, man?" asked Curtis.

"Why doh you mine yo own bitness, white boy?" asked the other guy.

White boy, is it? Hammock was a feist. He pushed back his chair and rose to continue the discourse, as did his counterpart at the other table. The cacophony in the lunchroom faded away, like it always does when a rumble is about to start. However, a professional aide noticed the confrontation and stopped it immediately.

"Sit down. *Botha* you. *Now!*" he said.

Hammock and the other guy slipped back into their seats with ugly faces. Each looked as if he'd been slapped by the other's words. The dispute was ended for the moment. Second period bell rang not too long afterwards. As the students filed out of the lunchroom at the end of First Period, Hammock and the black student began a wild street fight in the hallway outside, sliding on the polished linoleum floor and flailing at one another haphazardly with ineffective punches. It was over in less than 45 seconds, but the damage was done: the peace was broken. The uneasy calm exploded. By the end of the day, fights and a race riot erupted across both campuses.

Having said all this, let me interject that a half-century has come and gone. Memories, including mine, are growing hazy and in some cases, wiped clean. There is a Facebook group now with a thread of reminiscences about the riots claiming debilitating injuries, National Guard troops being called in, rape, and generalized mayhem. That all may be so, but most of it sounds like something that transpired in Minneapolis or Portland rather than in Gamecock City.

I don't think our recollections of the events are going to improve as the Class of '71 continues to age. But one thing is clear. The boy who got roughed up as bad or worse than anyone was Kurt Weatherly, a 16-year-old junior at Gamecock City High. As quiet and polite a guy as you would ever know, Kurt had an exceptional day. I remember Kurt well because I played in The Tempests, our soul band, with him for years. Also, his sister, Shawn, was Miss Universe.

An hour or two after Curtis Hammock's smack down outside the lunchroom, Kurt Weatherly was innocently leaving the same cafeteria and walking to class. To get to his class, he had to pass the school gym, which had become a social gathering place for black students. Some of them were quite angry. However, Weatherly knew none of this. He was just walking past with a friend. As they chatted, Kurt was grabbed and thrown on the wooden basketball court, face first. Blows rained down on his back, and someone began striking him with a desktop. Kurt could also hear people coming down the bleacher seats toward him.

Ronny Dixon, another student and trumpet player in the school band, ran to the office for help. Principal Bobby Matthews soon appeared and pulled Weatherly out of the gym.

As he tried to collect this thoughts and bearings, Kurt was told to go home, but he refused. Instead, he went to the principal's officer to be checked out by a nurse and interviewed by a policeman. Among his injuries, Weatherly developed bruises in a "T" shape from the beatings. Then he headed to class, thinking it was all over.

Not really.

While walking downstairs from the second floor, he came upon a large woman coming up the stairs with a knife. She looked him in the eyes, and in what became a school meme, she said, "I'm gonna cut you, white boy." With benefit of some judo training at Shaw Air Force Base, Weatherly kicked the woman in the chest and knocked her down to the wooden landing between the first and second floors.

What happened next was strange behavior from a quiet guy like Kurt Weatherly. He went home, got his .22-caliber single-shot rifle and some cartridges, and returned toward the school on foot. He didn't make it back to the campus with the rifle, thank God. Fifty years have elapsed, and Kurt doesn't remember why he didn't make it all the way to Gamecock High that day. As for the students who beat him up in the gym, no one was ever identified or prosecuted.

The chaos seemed to come and go in spurts thereafter. After an interlude, students roamed the halls, opening classroom doors and throwing smoke bombs inside. This was the "mob" that passed Mrs. McKay's English class where I was sitting and banged on the door windows. The glass windows were embedded with thin steel wires so there was no damage. School ended by mutual consent that day. I know of no one who was seriously injured, except arguably Kurt Weatherly and the girl with the knife that he'd kicked down on the stairs. There were undoubtedly fights on both campuses, though I have no documentation of specific instances on the other campus.

As for the property damage, *The Item* newspaper estimated it at around – you might want to sit down here – $400 give or take. When compared to the mobs of Portland, Oregon who showed up with flamethrowers and semi-automatic weapons, the Gamecock City High School "riot" was pretty mild.

The next day, Wednesday, would ultimately prove to be non-violent, but disorganized. When students first showed up, they had to walk through a massive cordon of police cruisers around the high schools. In another first for the Class of '71, this was probably the city's greatest congregation of law enforcement since 1865.

The Item's staff writer, Van King, under the headline "School Opens; Calm Prevails," reported the next day that, "[A]t least 60 Highway Patrolmen were called into town last night. [In addition,] police cars surrounded both campuses, and highway patrolmen cruised around the area." The Highway Patrolmen followed school buses to their stops. Classes ended until the following Monday.

Despite the heavy law enforcement presence, there's no documented record I could find of police brutality toward the students. Reverend Ralph Canty, Chairman of the Gamecock City School District Board of Trustees, described the relationship in the mid-1960s between black citizens and local law enforcement officers during Gamecock City's weekly civil rights marches as one of mutual respect. As Reverend Canty told *The Item*:

> *"[M]any communities responded with hostility…I still hold with awe a deep respect for Sheriff Parnell and Chief [of Police] Strange and Officer Priest and others; whatever their persuasions, they never took on the character of a Bull Conner or some of the other law enforcement people in the South."[2]*

Reverend Canty also noted that he worked for the Jackson family in Gamecock City and that they never complained or threatened him when he used his lunch hour to picket downtown stores. Surely there was anger on both sides of the race line, but there were no German shepherds or water cannons. As Reverend Canty observed, "Good people had been silent too long."

---

[2] *The Item, It Really Happened* at p. A7 (June 23, 2020) (commentary by Reverend Ralph Canty).

CHAPTER TWELVE

Ned Parker v. The Ku Klux Klan

A few weeks into the football season, on September 13, 1970 under a warm, South Carolina blue sky, I was collecting dust in a drugstore parking lot with some members of the football team, including Nedro, Cubman, Jimmy Brown (guitarist for The Tempests band), and a few others. The parking lot was a high school hangout. We were talking to one another through open car windows when a quick brace of activity caught our attention. Coming westward was a small line of pickup trucks and cars blowing their horns.

The lead vehicle was an El Camino pickup truck. It was a luxury truck, lime green and brown, with chrome wheel covers. A banner running across the side of the El Camino's cargo bed brandished the words: "Invisible Empire of the Ku Klux Klan." Drawn on white poster paper and affixed to the grille was the Klan's unique white cross with a drop of "pure" white blood in the center. Another poster duct-taped to the truck's rear quarter panel simply read "KKK." The poster was superfluous. We knew who these folks were. Everybody in Gamecock City knew about the Klan, although I didn't know anyone who actually claimed to be a member. I didn't realize the irony in the situation until years later: the KKK was parading down Liberty Street.

In the chaotic days of Reconstruction, the Klan included some members of Gamecock City's upper crust. As a child in the 1950s, I heard the KKK described by a few supposedly otherwise rational white people as a "necessary evil" during Reconstruction.

Although most of the Klan's hatred has been directed against blacks, the KKK's wrath was too broad to be delivered with surgical precision. By 1970, the Klan had revealed its true colors. Whatever its purported justification had been in the 1870s, the Klan had long-since expanded its target by the time the Class of '71 showed up for our senior year. The Klan's lists of *personae non gratae* included Jews, Catholics, immigrants from Eastern Europe, Asian Americans, homosexuals, Mexicans, and Native Americans.

The Klan wasn't the only organized group in Gamecock City. Possibly the most influential racist group in South Carolina was the Citizens' Council. It was the most important racist organization that the Class of '71 never heard of, though I suspect our parents at least knew of it.

Born in Indianoloa, Mississippi in 1954, Citizens' Councils had infiltrated South Carolina through Orangeburg County. Eventually, the Councils' membership in Mississippi grew to 80,000 and spread across the Southland. The Councils were growing rapidly in South Carolina as the Class of '71 grew to adulthood. Gamecock County had its own Citizens' Council by June of 1956.

Supposedly, the makeup of the Citizens Councils was different than that of the Klan. The Citizens' Council tried to recruit white professionals such as lawyers and doctors, powerful politicians, captains of industry, and the like. The Council took great pains to distance itself from the Ku Klux Klan with its violence and anti-Semitism. However, the Citizens' Councils had no love for black people. Their primary focus was to promote massive resistance to desegregation, and they were surely more effective at it than the Klan. The Citizens' Council had its own printing press which it used effectively to disseminate anti-desegregation propaganda.

But back to the "bad boys of racism."

• • •

As the El Camino rolled down Liberty Street, I saw a short and painfully skinny man in the truck bed wearing blue jeans. Deep sunburn/tan covered his arms where his white t-shirt sleeve ended. I guessed that he was probably a manual laborer. He wore a dour look on his face and had short hair held in a backwards swirl, courtesy of pomade. Hard, serious, and apparently poor, he was in his 50s or 60s. The skinny man never cast his deep-set eyes toward us, looking instead straight as a rifle shot down Liberty Street toward Second Mill. The man appeared down-right phlegmatic. He didn't seem to be a guy who'd make a public spectacle of himself by ranting and raving. There had to be some overarching reason why he was in this parade. He surely was an enigma to me.

The other men and boys in the El Camino weren't much to look at either. Except for the pickup truck and blue jeans, they could've been villeins on an oxcart headed to work on a lord's manor in medieval England, or Colonial-era draymen *en route* to market with a wagon load of squealing pigs. They smiled stupidly. The skinny man was enjoying what must've been one of the rare times in his life when he was a respected leader. For that moment, for that time, he was a general of infantry, a wizened chieftain to whose counsel all warriors obeyed unquestioningly.

The truck's white cardboard sign also announced that shortly, there was going to be a Klan rally at Gamecock County Speedway. Also known as "The Toughest Little Dirt Track in the South," the speedway was nearby, just outside the city limits on Highway 763 (a.k.a. the "Wedgefield Road"). It was in the high sheriff's jurisdiction.

Our sheriff, Ira Byrd Parnell, was the son of a lawman, and soon-to-be father of more lawmen. Although he could put the fear of the Lord in a white or black man's heart just to look at him, my father said the sheriff was a straight shooter who took pride in being a professional law enforcement officer, regardless of his private views (whatever those might have been). Gamecock City was never a wide-open, lawless town like Phenix City, Alabama or McNairy County, Tennessee. Parnell was president of the National Sheriff's Association and of his class at the FBI National School. He had closely cropped hair, eyeglasses with black rims above the eyes, a white panama hat with the brims rolled up, and wore an oxford shirt with a necktie. Nobody messed with this sheriff. He'd been head honcho for 18 years and told *The Washington Post* that he'd had no trouble with the Klan before that night.

"Y'all come on out!" shouted one of the other riders, happy as an oyster in pluff mud. "We gonna do some hangin' tonight."

Big talk. There had been times in South Carolina, most notably in the lynching era of 1882 to 1930, when white folks *could* actually murder black South Carolinians without resorting to that bothersome judicial process, but those days of midnight riders were gone by 1970, at least in Gamecock County.

Despite the happy demeanor of the younger men, the skinny man's mind seemed affixed on "righting wrongs" and reversing the tide of change sweeping through our flat, sandy county. He was in no humor to make light of the situation. Like a squadron of German Stuka bombers headed for Lódz, the parade vanished down Liberty Street toward the speedway.

• • •

The Ku Klux Klan's name is taken from the Greek word *kuklos*, which means circle, and the English word clan, as in the Scottish clans. The Klan's infamous burning cross was adopted by the KKK's founders from the Highland Scots' legendary fiery crosses, which were sent by runners or horsemen through the countryside, a sign that indicated the clans were required to come defend against an attack, usually by another Scottish clan or the English. Not that the Scots had any say in the matter of their heritage being used by the KKK.

The Klan started innocently enough. It was a sort of fraternity in Pulaski, Tennessee, for ex-Confederate soldiers created by Confederate Lieutenant General Nathan Bedford Forrest. A sturdy man sporting a black goatee, Forrest was one of the Civil War's fiercest, most tactically brilliant, and ruthless cavalry generals. As a lieutenant general, Forrest was a killing machine and a natural leader of men. Various records show that he personally killed over thirty Union troops with a saber, shotgun, or pistol. His troops took 31,000 prisoners. Said by some to have been the Confederacy's greatest cavalry officer, Forrest had been a fabulously wealthy plantation owner and slave trader before the war.

He wasn't happy about losing to the Yankees, and Forrest turned the Klan into a paramilitary terrorist organization that wreaked havoc until it went into remission after Congress enacted statutes allowing the use of federal troops to pursue Klansmen in 1870 and 1871.

The Klan spread to South Carolina a few years after the Civil War as a counter to the Union League, a society founded with the mission to support the Union and Abraham Lincoln's policies. The South Carolina Klan was most powerful in the upcountry's twelve western-most districts, especially in Chester, Laurens, and Spartanburg.

The carpetbagger legislature could not handle the Klan. After all, only 881 federal troops remained in the state by 1868, and the Klan could never have been effectively dealt with by so few Union soldiers in an area covering 31,189 square miles of land and water. Things got out of control, so much so that carpetbagger Governor Scott had to request that former C.S.A. General Wade Hampton speak out to avoid a race war. Hampton quickly appealed for preservation of order. The Klan returned to its lair.

As children, my great-great grandfather Robbie Blanding and his sister, Madge, imagined the Klan as their worst nightmare – akin to terrible ghosts and demons who haunted the night. There's a family story that one day while they were being too rambunctious on the playground swings, Robbie and Madge began to loudly sing:

"The Ku Klux'll catch ya if you don't be good!

The Ku Klux'll catch ya if you don't be good!"

Their mother, to her horror, heard them chanting and called out to the children from the dining room window:

"Children, stop singing that. The Ku Klux Klan might hear you!"

Robbie and Madge crept into the house and hid behind closed doors lest the night riders come.

Early Klansmen didn't wear pointed hats or white robes, which purportedly represented ghosts of slain Confederate soldiers, although they did wear masks. They also didn't carry skulls in their saddles, which happened in later years. The Klansmen nonetheless were a vicious group that specialized in bullying defenseless former slaves and freemen, their wives, their children, and white "race traitors." Since Reconstruction, the KKK has been terrorizing America in one place or another. Whenever racial conflict arises, so does the Klan.

This wasn't the first time I had crossed paths with the KKK. A friend of mine showed up at McLaurin Junior High School one day with a Klan patch on his blue jean jacket, but he was neither in the Klan, nor was his family connected to it. I don't know where he got the Klan patch. After some flack, he never wore it again.

• • •

However, even in my arrested stage of intellectual development, seeing a Klan rally firsthand was intriguing. I turned to some of the other guys sitting around in the parking lot that fall Sunday:

"Wanta go, guys?" I asked them.

The Klansmen didn't look so tough to me. In fact, most of the young goofballs on the truck seemed to be enjoying all this. Happy boys. I suspected my buddies were up for a bit of adventure. My parents would've had coronaries if they knew we were planning to go to the speedway to see a Klan rally. The Klansmen were supposed to be virulent Jew haters after all, but hey, they'd never know who my grandfather was.

"Yeah, let's," Cub said.

Being young and feeling invincible, I put the Ford into drive, and off we went. At Nedro's house, we transferred to his Pontiac GTO. Some of the others went in their own cars. As it turned out, we were about to get in over our heads. This was no ordinary Klan rally. Before the night was over, there would be mayhem and murder at the Gamecock City Speedway.

• • •

The entrance to the Gamecock County Speedway was on a two-lane blacktop. Built in 1954 and already aging in 1970, Gamecock County Speedway is a 3/8-mile oval dirt racetrack. Its large, flat parking lot is both unpaved and un-landscaped. That afternoon a four-foot high plywood stage had been erected in the center of the lot. Standing on the highway at the entrance directing traffic with what looked like long, white police flashlights were two or three nighthawks. A nighthawk is a Klan security officer, sometimes attired in black robes and hoods. (These nighthawks looked like they'd been directing traffic all their lives, but that's a purely subjective observation on my part.) Inside, the parking lot was beginning to fill. The nighthawk waved us in, and our cars bounced along the rutted path to a parking area. The warm afternoon had lapsed into a nippy evening.

"You wanta get out the car or just watch from here?" Jimmy asked, a bit apprehensive about the whole thing.

"Let's get out," I said.

I believed without question that no harm would befall us. After all, weren't we white males? Who's safer at a Klan rally than a white male? So long as I didn't pull out a yarmulke and we kept our mouths shut, that is. We hopped out and wandered about, but there wasn't much to see really. Following a desultory path around the parking lot were a few men dressed in white Klan outfits. I suspect that most of the other Klansmen who were attending were in mufti. On the stage was a man addressing the crowd over a public address system.

"Welcome folks," he chirped magnanimously. "Over here by the left side of the stage is a concession stand with food prepared by good white Christian hands."

Also being sold in the concession stand was good white Christian beer in plastic cups. A band dressed in white satin outfits began to play on stage. It looked like a family band, the type you'd see at a Pentecostal tent-revival meeting, though I certainly do not mean to imply any connection whatso*ever* between Pentecostals and the Klan. Some of the musicians were children. The musical group wasn't a tight, hard-hitting gospel band like the Statesmen or some of the other more prominent vocal quartets. They were just country folks. They played through pretty good equipment, though – Fender guitars, Fender amps, Slingerland drums, and a bright red Kustom 200 PA system. In between songs, polemics and venom were tossed out by Klansmen who stepped up to the mike. Otherwise, it was quite low key. Certainly not Hitler screaming to the Nazi party faithful at the Nuremberg Rallies.

There was, however, more to this Klan rally than met the eye. A quiet storm had been rising since Robert E. Scoggin, Grand Dragon of the United Klans of America, South Carolina Realm, and his boss man, Imperial Wizard Robert Shelton of Alabama, were tossed into the federal pen. The Imperial Wizard and Grand Dragon had refused to turn over Klan membership lists, and the House Committee on Un-American Activities tossed them in jail for contempt. Before being incarcerated at a federal prison in La Tuna, Texas, Scoggin handed over his title of Grand

Dragon, apparently with the understanding that he would get it back once he was released. But Scoggin was betrayed.

Robert Echols Scoggin (his Polk County, North Carolina birth certificate reads "Robert Eckles Scoggins") was a driven man. As a teenager, he worked in Spartanburg, South Carolina's Beaumont Textile Mill as a head doffer, replacing full spindles of thread with empty ones. Hitler rejuvenated Germany's economy, Mussolini got Italian trains running on time, and like most bad men, Scoggin wasn't "entirely bad," at least not as his children tell his story. Cigarette-thin and redneck handsome, Scoggin was a World War II veteran who'd served his country in the Coast Guard as a cook. When the ship was under attack, Coxswain Scoggin manned an anti-aircraft gun. His son recalls that the two ships on which Scoggin served were sunk. In one sea battle, Scoggin was wounded. He received a Purple Heart for his injury. After an honorable discharge in 1945, he reenlisted in 1950, then became a civilian. Scoggin learned the plumber's trade and began working in Spartanburg County to support his wife and children.

He struggled to regain power upon release from prison. Three months before Gamecock County's KKK rally, he incorporated a new group in South Carolina called the "Invisible Empire of the Knights of the Ku Klux Klan." Comprised of Klansmen largely from the upstate, Scoggin's Invisible Empire was sponsoring the rally we were attending at the Gamecock County Speedway. Also attending were Scoggin's enemies – members of his former United Klans of America. Sheriff Parnell was there to keep watch. It was a gathering of men who were comfortable with violence.

The fireworks had yet to start at the KKK rally, and so far, my friends and I were unimpressed. We had no quarrel with black people. Ninety-nine percent of trouble in our daily lives was caused by white people. However, Nedro, intellectual that he is, became aggravated. He wanted to debate. He *loved* to argue and was good at it. Nedro purposely strode up to a man decked out in a white robe to engage him in dispassionate, reasoned debate. Right off the bat, Nedro got sarcastic.

The Klansman was not, like Nedro, dispassionate. He was emotionally wrapped up in the "inferiority of the Negro race" and "the evil Jews," and it was important to him that everyone agree on this point. Gamecock County Speedway was the hooded man's turf that evenin'. The man was unappreciative of what he perceived to be a city boy's superciliousness and insolence. As strange as it might seem, poorer folks in Gamecock County apparently considered us to be refined, though we were just redneck boys ourselves. Anyway, the Klansman got riled up.

Nedro was no wispy geranium. It's true that he wasn't real tall, just about 5 feet 10 inches or so, but he was as solid as the tractors on his daddy's farm in Eastover where he'd worked summers since he was a child. He had sandy blond hair and a defensive tackle's compact body strengthened by lifting weights. Nedro was not used to backing down. The man facing him was not nearly as strong and certainly lacked Nedro's stamina, but there was an armed posse surrounding us, and we were slipping into deep yogurt.

"Boy, you some kind of *nig*guh lover?" the Klansman snarled. "What you doing out here anyways? You friends with them *nig*guhs?"

Now, there's a fine line between insane and heroic. If so, I'd like to think that Ned was in the latter category. The reality though was that we were five high school kids surrounded by many, many Klansmen and their families and having had our say, we needed to leave. Now. To this day, I remember Ned's reply:

"Yeah, we friends with 'em. And we like 'em better'n *you!*"

Now, I've seen some angry people in my life, but I've *never* seen a look like the one on that Klansman's face (and he was wearing a hood and a robe). His blood bubbled with anger — pure rage mitigated neither by reason nor compassion. Drawn by the argument, more Klansmen and their sympathizers had surrounded us. They weren't beauty pageant contestants either. Nedro was trying to get a few narrow points across, which were answered with white-trash verbal retorts. The Klansmen's replies usually began with something like: "You can kiss my big, white..." or "I don't give a flying..."

It might as well have been a colloquy between a man and a pig. Nedro succeeded in changing no one's philosophy, no one's view of world history, and no one's politics. However, he did succeed in putting the entire Klavern into one gigantic bad mood. We were in danger of taking a fearful and brutal gang beating that would've made a Cossack blush or an SS trooper glow with pride.

Had a black man stood underneath the lights arguing in that dirt parking lot like Nedro was doing, the Klansmen might not have become so undone so fast, but a white boy refusing to stand by his *own* race? Now that's a whole 'nother matter. Nothing incites the Klan to anger like the perceived disloyalty of a race traitor. Meanwhile, I was searching with my eyes trying to see where our cars were parked.

The arguing continued, and it was about to get real physical.

"Then I got somethin' you can talk about, son," injected a man standing nearby.

The fellow stepped up close to Ned. Mischief was afoot. Despite his slight build and lack of a Klan robe, the man had fox eyes. He was sidlin' up to Nedro for the classic Gamecock County sucker punch.

It was then that a tiny woman in a satin dress came through the crowd. She walked up to Nedro. This woman probably had seen the gathering from the stage where she'd been performing with the family band. She'd hopped down and strode over to the commotion. Her hair was clean but long, coarse and stringy. It was streaked with grey, no doubt the fashion of her youth. Her satin dress fit like a sack, which was appropriate because the woman's short, squat body had the curves of a baked potato. Standing beside her, utterly silent yet baleful and agitated, was the skinny man from the El Camino.

The speedway parking lot was dark and shadow-cast by now. The weak lights were augmented by some flickering torches, and to this day, I can still smell their dusky smoke. I saw no one notable present, such as a prominent official, but there were a *lot* of people out there. This was undeniably one of those periodic incoming tides of social change when the Klan tends to put muscle on its skeleton. The ghostly Klansmen in their white robes had the same effect upon these poor Gamecock County folk as had the Druid priests on English country people in the shires of centuries past performing pagan rituals.

The diminutive lady looked up at Nedro with a pinched face. Dry, wrinkled gullies in her skin ran from underneath her nose down to her thin lips. She held her gaze on him for a full ten seconds. Hers were the unornate, leather-framed eyes of a timeless peasant woman, eyes that would quietly mist at the sight of a roadside-stand velvet Jesus or bear a raw hole in an urchin grandchild who's grown too boisterous at church. I couldn't read her heart, but certainly a crucible was transpiring inside it. Her loving, forgiving Christian faith was in a desperate hand-to-hand struggle with the Klan goodwife terrorist in her soul. Both adversaries in her inner conflict were formidable opponents. One wanted the woman to wrap her arms around bright-eyed Nedro like her own child and scream at the men of the mob to leave the boy alone. The other, bristling with hatred, yearned to proclaim *ecce homo* and let the mob's will be done. The Klan dignitaries showed her deference. She must have been a mother, grandmother, aunt, or cousin to one or more of them.

"Yessum?" Nedro asked as she approached.

The little woman peered directly at 17-year-old Nedro, a sheltered, yet brave boy. She looked around at the faces in the crowd. Then, she met the eyes of the skinny man from the El Camino who had opened his mouth to speak but thought better of it. Finally, she turned back to Nedro, standing vulnerably in the center of the circle of Klansmen.

"Son, I don't know who you are or whur you come from, but you ain't welcome here nuh-more. If you don't leave, these here boys is gonna hurt you. It's high time you get in your car and go home to your momma."

When the woman said "momma," everyone understood that she intended neither a slight on his manhood nor a cheap joke, but that she had a vision of Nedro's mother waiting at home for her son to return and the sadness a mother feels when her boy is hurt. No one dared move or speak. All eyes were on the woman.

"Boy, you hear me talkin'?" she asked.

Nedro just stared at her.

With no response forthcoming by Nedro, and having seen too much negotiating and not enough action, one of the round-faced men in the crowd burst out, "I'm gonna kick your behind, city boy, you..."

"No *suh!*" shouted the woman, instantly rotating her head on that fleshy, stubby neck and looking the round-faced man dead in the eye. It was the voice of an aunt who'd raised her nephew from a child and still expected absolute obedience, even though the nephew was close to 45-years-old and as big as a pontoon boat. He lowered his eyes, shamed.

"Nedro, she makes a lot of sense," I interjected.

Nedro's argumentative brain was just about to push another smart-headed remark through his mouth. These fellows were not going to take lightly any perceived insult to this woman, whoever she was. They wanted blood on their knuckles, something to show their coworkers at work the next morning. Still, the woman's mere presence held back the meaty ring of men and boys dwarfing her.

"You ain't gonna change anybody's mind here tonight, Nedro," I said again.

The skinny man and the old woman stood immobile like two satin dwarfs. Even the crowd outside of the circle was silent. Nedro looked up toward the flickering torchlights burning above us all and slumped.

Nedro finally replied softly, "Yes ma'am," and turned back to his car. Before Ned could get to the car, a Klansman grabbed his arm. It was a nighthawk.

"You ain't goin' nowheres 'til you 'pologize, boy," he shouted.

Nedro looked at him and saw a crowd of angry men gathering around again. The Klansman jerked him onto the ground. Some of the men threw beer on him. His knees on the ground, Ned looked up. His face and clothes were wet with draft beer. Nedro, even then a master of the graceful sidestep, said: "Okay! I *apol*ogize," with an insolent look on his face.

It was a good thing he did, or ol' Nedro might not be building houses in sunny Southern California today. Killing was in the air that night. He pushed himself up from the dirt with the palms of his hands and walked toward his GTO. The final round of debate was unilateral. It consisted of Nedro's counterparts throwing more cups of beer on us as we leisurely walked to his car, attempting to reclaim some dignity with our controlled pace; it didn't work very well. However, we did make it out of the Gamecock County Speedway alive.

• • •

A few days later, Jimmy Brown and I went over to Nedro's house near Swan Lake, one of Gamecock City's parks. Ned's parents lived in what was generally accepted as the rich side of town. He was lying on his bed reading a Superman comic book while Mahler played on his audiotape cassette player. Nedro sure seemed to be going through an uppity phase for a Gamecock City High School defensive tackle.

"You hear what happened after we left that rally?" Nedro asked.

"No, tell me," I said.

"You know Mr. Odom from Odom's Grocery Store? He got his brains blown out by one of those Klan nighthawks," Nedro replied. "Someone brought a tape recorder to the rally, and the KKK wanted to confiscate it. There was a fight and shooting broke out."

According to the *Washington Post* and the *New York Times*, the dead man was a member of the rival United Klans of America, which had refused to give Robert Scoggin his Grand

Dragonship back after Scoggin's release from prison in January 1970. Odom had been shot in the back of his head with a .38 pistol while driving out of the rally. Mr. Odom himself had fired six .22 pistol shots beforehand. His wife later said, however, that Mr. Odom fired the shots into the air.

He died instantly. His wife and children were in the car with Mr. Odom and were injured when the car crashed into a ditch. Another United Klans of America infiltrator had his face and body bloodied after he refused to surrender the tape recorder. When the suspected witnesses were asked who had committed the crimes, they refused to answer. Then they drove away from the speedway against Sheriff Parnell's instructions.

Oddly enough, Willie Odom was quite well known by some students in the Class of '71. He'd owned a grocery store on Lafayette Drive called Odom's Grocery. Mr. Odom's employee had been known to sell a quart bottle of Pabst Blue Ribbon beer to any boy who was tall enough to see over the countertop beside the cash register. For that reason, he would be greatly missed by students about town. I'm sure none of the students knew he was a Klansman, if he actually was one.

The *Washington Post* reported Parnell's quote about not having any issues with the Klan in the 18 years since he was elected. The *New York Times* also reported on the killings, but only *The Item*, Gamecock City's local daily newspaper, followed the case to the bitter end. Ten indictments were handed down, all of which involved men from outside Gamecock County.

• • •

Solicitor Kirk McLeod, the prosecutor, was a capable trial lawyer. Sure, he was known to flare up at times, a victim of his fiery temper, but he was regarded in Gamecock County as a fair man. Prosecuting criminals was low-key stress compared to what he had done in the Army Air Corps, having received the Distinguished Flying Cross for flying 65 combat missions in World War II. Like most good prosecutors, McLeod brought his strongest case first, which was against the nighthawk who supposedly had killed Mr. Odom.

As often the case with a masked man, everything turned on identification of the shooter. Some folks developed memory problems. Another witness was shot dead before trial. Solicitor McLeod could not establish identity, at least not to the satisfaction of Charleston County Judge John Grimball, who was riding the circuit through Gamecock County when court proceedings began on November 9, 1971. The judge had to dismiss the charges.

Parnell and McLeod were unhappy, but facts are stubborn things. Nobody can identify a shooter's face hidden underneath a Klan robe. Grand Dragon Robert Scoggin was in the courtroom to support and encourage the nighthawk. Scoggin was terribly pleased by the dismissal. He vowed to fight against Sheriff Parnell and Solicitor McLeod in the next election. Both the sheriff and prosecutor were reelected anyway.

One wonders if undue pressure were put on Judge Grimball to dismiss the case. After all, violence wasn't unheard of in a Gamecock City courtroom. It's hard to forget Judge "Tuck" Haynsworth who'd been shot and killed there when gunfire broke out. Haynsworth was a national hero of the Confederacy, and if Judge Haynsworth could be shot, *any*one could be killed there.

But knowing the tenacity of Grimball lawyers firsthand, having practiced law at Grimball and Cabaniss, LLC, for 31 years, I'd make book that Judge Grimball would never have buckled under any pressure, even assuming he'd been personally threatened. Those Grimballs can be quite hardheaded.

• • •

Many decades have passed since that warm, sepia-lensed Sunday when I saw that parade swoop by on Liberty Street. The Southern Poverty Law Center tells me that there's no record of

Klan activity in Gamecock County over the last couple of years, but it's just a matter of time.

Thinking back on that night, I sometimes wonder about the skinny man and what impregnated him with so much acrimony. Was it a single event that, like the bite of a stray dog, punctured deeply to draw the blood of hated, or was it instead a series of events in his life that pushed him over the tailgate into the bed of that pickup truck to become a proponent of racial discontent in Gamecock County? Had a gang of black kids bloodied his nose in front of his girlfriend when they were youngsters, humiliating him? Did the boss man on his jobsite anoint a black man as the new foreman, passing over the skinny man like Coach Jack Williams, jilted in his desire to be head coach, who'd felt it was his turn? Or was his bias against people who were different than him a legacy handed down over the ages in the oral tradition? Most of all, I wonder about the skinny man's wife and what they said to one another about Nedro as they made their way home on that haunted fall night so many years ago.

But none of the racial anger and resentment besetting the Class of '71 had left such pain and sadness as Gamecock City's most deadly citizen – Donald H. ("Pee Wee") Gaskins, Jr.

CHAPTER THIRTEEN

Pee Wee

"I need to tell you a little about [Gamecock City]. It's not a big town. Everybody pretty much knows who everybody else is, though there is layers of folks who don't have nothing to do with those living on different layers – like I reckon things is most everywhere. For the most part, people speak to one another and are friendly and polite."

Donald H. Gaskins, Jr.

Desegregation wasn't the only jolting thing happening to the Class of '71. There was Pee Wee.

Donald Henry Gaskins, Jr., best known to the world as "Pee Wee," used to mail cartoons with love notes to people across the state, including Jack Swerling's pretty blonde paralegal, who trashed them. It was part of a scam Gaskins was pulling to make money from his prison cell on death row. Pee Wee was a serial killer Jack had represented. I worked for Jack Swerling as a law clerk, though, blessedly, I had nothing to do with Pee Wee or his case.

Some would say that Gaskins made serial killer Larry Gene Bell look like Mother Teresa. The argument could also be made that, compared to Pee Wee, Jack the Ripper, Ted Bundy, John Wayne Gacy, and Jeffrey Dahmer were amateurs. Crime author Colin Wilson called Gaskins "the worst serial killer of all time," and if half of what Pee Wee claimed in his autobiography is correct, Wilson is right.

You might say that he was evil perfected. It's as if the Devil had waited millennia to find the perfect vessel to fill with evil. Pee Wee was angry that after his tortures, rapes, and murders of all those young girls and boys, he never got the national press he deserved. And though I had no direct connection with Pee Wee's criminal prosecution, the Class of '71 had *far* too much in common with him.

Gaskins was born in neighboring Florence County to an uninterested daddy. But Pee Wee himself was a family man of sorts: he was "married" many times. Most of the marriages were bigamous, however, because he never divorced his first wife.

Pee Wee was just one of his nicknames. They also called him the "Meanest Man in America" and the "Redneck Charles Manson." Gaskins had dark hair and not an entirely uncomely face. In his youth, Pee Wee was handsome despite the fact that, physically-speaking, he was a shrimp. In some photographs, Pee Wee could pass for country music singer Little Jimmy Dickens, if you put a ten-gallon cowboy hat on him and don't look too closely. Gaskins seemed to kill for just about any reason: anger, boredom, sex, resentment, or money. He was flexible that way. Pee Wee called this desire to kill his "bothersomeness."

Most people have had some form of murderous fantasy at some point in their life. What made Gaskins different from the rest of us was that he wasn't afraid to kill. He could pull the trigger. And once he lost the fear of murdering and realized the power this gave him over ordinary people like us, he could get almost anything he wanted.

You might say that Gaskins went to high school with the Class of '71, because he haunted Gamecock County from our sophomore through our senior years, killing when he felt like it. Stories about missing local girls and hitchhikers peppering our local media were his doing.

• • •

In November of 1968, Pee Wee was paroled from Central Correctional Institute ("CCI") in Columbia. It was South Carolina's most desperate prison. CCI stood like a tombstone under an eternal dark cloud and was surrounded by barbed wire, reminding Columbians driving by that there was another awful parallel universe into which they might be sucked, if they don't obey the policeman.

Gaskins got his personal effects that fall of 1968, walked out of the prison's gate, and headed straight down Highway 378 to Gamecock City. Once he got to town, Pee Wee took a liking to the place, so he decided to stay awhile.

Great.

Now, *he* was a character. For example, part of his time in Gamecock County, Pee Wee drove around town in a hearse. There was a card in the back that read "We haul anything – living or dead." The local law enforcement agencies didn't take him seriously, not for a long time. After all, he was just a tiny, big-talking guy. Nothing but mouth, right? Nope. And South Carolina would regret this.

Initially, Pee Wee lived around Gamecock County in trailers (he seemed to eschew the pretentious new term "mo-bile home") with Gamecock City women. He later rented a trailer on Boulevard Road and after that, a house on Manning Avenue, but much of his mayhem transpired at an old sharecropper shack in Concord, an area crossed by Highway 378 and the Brewington Road. It was near my grandfather's farm where my brothers, sisters, parents, and I lived for a while in the 1950s. Pee Wee called the sharecropper shack his "tenant house."

No one had a clue that the girls disappearing in Gamecock City and along the coast were being murdered by Pee Wee. Many of them were hitchhikers from other states whose parents didn't even know their daughters were traveling through South Carolina. Some girls were quite affluent. They had hundreds of dollars in their pockets to pay for transportation. Others were showing their "independence" by hitchhiking, as was done in the spirit of those times. Gaskins liked independent girls.

The Law could never catch him. That is, not until his best friend, Walter Neely, told his minister about Pee Wee. By this time, Gaskins had fired a Beretta into the brain of Diane, Walter's 29-year-old wife, and buried her in a grave near Alligator Landing.

Gamecock City didn't learn about most of the bodies until years later. He'd buried many of them behind his tenant house and others in the Neck, these days a hip "habitat" in which to kayak. Eventually, Pee Wee told the Law about them so the prosecutor would agree not to seek the death penalty.

Gaskins was a roofer and a mechanic by trade. A while after he rolled into Gamecock City from prison, he got a job at Fort Roofing and Sheet Metal Works on West Oakland Street. Fort Roofing worked on Gamecock City's schools. This led to his most famous crime.

As Pee Wee told it in his book, *Final Truth*, he'd just climbed down off a roof and was going to a work truck for some supplies when young Peggy Cuttino, daughter of Gamecock City's powerful state representative, walked by with a friend. Some believe that he'd been working on the new YMCA under construction, but Pee Wee implied he'd been at a school, possibly Willow Drive School. She didn't attend school there but was unlucky enough to be at the wrong place at the wrong time. Gaskins said hello to Peggy, and she supposedly replied that he was white trash. This made Pee Wee angry.

Pee Wee claims he kidnaped and murdered her. The problem with all this is that another man, Junior Pierce, was convicted of the crime. Gaskins confessed to killing Peggy Cuttino, but his confession wasn't accepted. This led to great controversy and anger at the law enforcement officials involved. Sheriff Parnell who, before Gaskins' confession, virtually walked on water in Gamecock County, was given his walking papers by the voters. Prosecutor Kirk McLeod got his too.

Pee Wee quit Fort Roofing and got a job at a used-car lot literally across the tracks on Manning Avenue. He worked as a mechanic there. At night, he went out drinking at nearby honkytonks and low-rent lounges. Gaskins also drove to Sam's Nightclub in nearby Lake City. He liked to hang out on Gamecock City's Broad Street Extension at what he called "The Drive Inn Restaurant," which was likely Cole's Drive-In or Big Jim's Drive-In. Gaskins drove the same streets and highways as my schoolmates and I, except Pee Wee was looking for young girls and boys to torture, rape, and murder.

Our senior year at Gamecock High School, Gaskins murdered his own sister's pretty, blonde, 15-year-old daughter Janice Kirby, a Gamecock City High School sophomore. He also killed her friend Patricia Ann ("Patty") Alsbrooks, a fresh-faced member of the Class of '71 with eyeglasses and long, beautiful brown hair. Uncle Pee Wee picked them up at The Drive Inn Restaurant. After driving them to his tenant shack, he tried to rape his niece. When Pee Wee was unsuccessful (Patty fought like a tiger, smacking Pee Wee in his head with a two-by-four at one point), he beat in their skulls with the stock of his pistol. One week, Patty and Janice walked the school hallways with us. The next day Patty was at the bottom of a septic tank in Gamecock County and Janice was in a shallow grave. There they remained for years.

He wasn't prosecuted, at least not then. Pee Wee had admitted to the girls' families and the Law that Janice and Patty had gotten into his car that evening. However, he said he had let the two girls out, and they'd gotten into another vehicle with some Orangeburg boys. Gaskins claimed Janice and Patty had been talkin' about running away to California. That was the end of that. Who knew?

• • •

Gaskins started stretching out. He left Gamecock County, sometimes before daylight, and drove to the coastal highways to pick up girls and boys, then rape and murder them. In his book *Final Truth*, Pee Wee claimed that typically he first tortured his victims, often in creative ways. He burned some with acid. One girl he pumped full of water. Gaskins cut off body parts then fed them back to the victims. He rammed his Arkansas Toothpick, a long-bladed stiletto, into their body openings. After they were dead, or barely alive, the girls were drowned with their hands tied behind their backs. In his inimitable way, Gaskins called his murders of these girls and boys "coastal kills." The key for Gaskins was to torture the victims in such a way that they didn't die too soon. One girl held on for four days.

During the Class of '71's senior year of high school, Gaskins claimed he was making a kill about once every six weeks. Mostly he killed white folks, young girls to be specific. However, he ascribed to some of the KKK's beliefs, too. One black woman, Martha Ann "Clyde" Dicks, he killed in his tenant shack because she claimed she was pregnant with Pee Wee's child. Clyde came one time too many to Gaskin's job site on Manning Avenue, talking trash among the other employees about Gaskins. But what finally got Gaskins executed was murdering another prison inmate with a bomb. All in all, Pee Wee disposed of as many as 80 to 100 bodies in swamps, freshly dug graves, and septic tanks.

Or so he claims. Some of the murders he surely did. Gamecock County Deputy Sheriff (and later Sheriff) Tommy Mims worked on the prosecution of another notorious killer in the county, Junior Pierce. I called him in December of 2010 from my car to see what he thought about all of this. Sheriff Mims recalls Gaskins quite clearly, including his hearse, but he believes Pee Wee lied about the number of people he killed in Gamecock County. Sheriff Mims saw Gaskins as manipulative and slick, a liar and conniver who made up things to make himself look big. Taking credit for killing so many other victims was just another way to ingratiate himself and give himself notoriety, believed Sheriff Mims. Nor did he think Gaskins committed all of the coastal kills he claimed.

The Law finally caught up with Gaskins on Main Street in Gamecock City. He had just mailed off his foot-long Arkansas Toothpick stiletto (presumably to himself) to hide it, but the Law was already closing in on him. Pee Wee was in a taxicab leaving the post office *en route* to the bus station. He planned to flee south to Savannah. Suddenly, the area was flooded with cops who pulled him from the taxi. A local businessman had identified him.

• • •

On his execution day, Pee Wee was asked if he had any final words. With a smiling face, he told his lawyer, "I'm ready to go!" Pee Wee was in good company because a whole lot of people in Gamecock County and across South Carolina were ready for him to go, too. Devil worshipers had been writing to him and wanted to use his grave as a meeting place, so he asked to be cremated. Shirley Gaskins, his dutiful daughter, complied with her daddy's wishes. In the back of his book is a picture of her in some desolate spot near dead trees. She's holding a clear plastic bag with his ashes as she prepares to throw them onto the ground. And in a touch of the weird that Gaskins surely would've appreciated, there's a "Pee Wee Gaskins Band" in South Jakarta, Indonesia. Unfortunately for Gaskins, he never caught on with the public like those other high-profile serial killers. Sorry, Pee Wee.

Our family inadvertently got drawn into the Gaskins mix twice. My father got a call from the police in the early 1970s. Apparently, my brother Ben had sold one of our dad's cars to Pee Wee, not knowing who he was. Pee Wee never re-registered the car in his own name, and it was found abandoned in the woods, possibly in connection with one of Gaskins' evil deeds.

It happened again on Christmas Break. Each year, the men in our family and friends have a campout in December.

On December 19th, 1970, the campout was held in the woods beside the Brewington Road. My big brother Mike sent Curtis Hammock, Nedro Parker, Essex Durant, the Cub, and me on a "search-and-destroy mission." Our assignment? Arrest a road-side Speed Limit 35 sign, take it into custody, and bring it back to camp.

In our zeal to be the first team to accomplish our mission, we set off with high-pitched cackling, screaming, and yelling. I imagine we sounded like a girl screaming. Curtis and I yanked up a road sign and were merrily running with it down the Brewington Road when the night suddenly turned blue from the revolving lights of police cruisers. My venerable brother (he was 25-years-old) decided to deal with the incident in a mature and professional way: he jumped into a ditch alongside the road when the police cars first began sliding to a stop, and there he hunkered down.

After a few minutes of soaking in the ditch, Mike decided to take the matter into his own hands. He climbed out, went to speak to the officers, and gave them our home phone number. A law enforcement officer promptly called my father: "Yes, sir. Sorry to wake you. We have several young men who set up a campsite in some woods beside the Brewington Road. Sir, it appears to be on your property."

"Officer, they're my sons and some of their friends," said my dad. "Are they breaking the law?"

"No sir. They're just out here running down the road, hoopin' and hollerin'. We have a missing person report and wanted to confirm that they're your people."

"Okay."

"And two of them are in a ditch with a Speed Limit 35 sign."

"Yes, officer. That sounds like my boys."

"Thank you, sir. We'll be moving on."

According to my dad, he rolled over and went back to sleep. We couldn't figure out why the entire Gamecock City and County law enforcement agencies were so concerned about two happy-faced high school seniors borrowing a speed limit sign, nor why they let us go after catching us red-handed. No one even made us give the stop sign back.

We later learned that the officers suspected us to have been poor Peg Cuttino screaming in the woods. Pee Wee's tenant shack was not far away, just down the Brewington Road. She'd been kidnapped the day before.

CHAPTER FOURTEEN

Boots on the Ground - the New York Times Invades

B y November of 1970, the school administrators and the students were still taking it day-by-day. There was suspicion between the two camps, especially by some of the former Lincoln High School students. For example, an audience with the School Board was requested by several black students and a former Lincoln High faculty member. The idea was to rap a bit and try to bridge the gap between former Edmunds High students and former Lincoln High students.

I wasn't there, but according to Superintendent McArthur's memoir, "Six black . . . students – Wilbert Robins, Yulaundra Ferguson, Howard McFaddin, Wanda Wells, Yvonne McFadden, and James Weeks[, plus] Robert L. Jefferson[, history teacher and advisor to the Black Heritage Club,] presented six concerns and also suggestions for ameliorating the concerns." These students wanted measures taken to make former Lincolnites at the Haynsworth Street Campus feel more at home. The measures included adding more black male staffers to the Haynsworth Street campus. Moreover, they advocated correcting the "demotion of all black men in leadership capacities, such as principals, band, football, and basketball coaches."

There were other issues too, according to Dr. McArthur. The group believed that because former Lincolnite students were forced to give up their school name, their mascot, and were made to relinquish other important symbols, more concessions should be made by the School Board. These included removing the Edmunds statue and anything else bearing the name "Edmunds," erasing the undue influence of biased parents and police, mandatory sensitivity training seminars, and establishment of a "student investigating committee."

Anyway, the school board thanked the black students and Coach Jefferson for coming to the meeting. Next on the agenda was a group of white students, who, according to Dr. McArthur, included Joe Albritton, Kevin McGinnis, Julie Summers, Cindy Taylor, and Kathleen Kirby. One or more members of this group was equally disgruntled. They wanted the elimination of weapons on campus, improvement of transportation between the two campuses, an end to class disruptions, and (my favorite) a request for fewer fire drills. One or more members of the white contingent also brought up a need for improvements in attitude and better discipline, namely threats, ganging up on one another, painting on the walls and other vandalism in the bathrooms, theft, and scattering of garbage in the cafeteria. Someone also voiced unhappiness with black power symbols on jackets or shirts because black power symbols had been made disciplinary violations and banned, along with the Confederate flag and the playing of *Dixie*.

• • •

Into this mix came Roy Reed and Paul Delaney, reporters for the *New York Times*. They wrote an article "on the basis of two weeks reporting in [Gamecock City, South Carolina], and discussions over many months with officials, students, and parents 'in the South.'" It was published on the front page of the *New York Times* back in its heyday on April 18, 1971. The article was entitled *Year of Desegregation: [A] Trying One in South.*

Cat-eyed with black hair that appeared as if it'd been doused with Brylcreem and looking younger than his 40 years, Reed was a respected news reporter. He covered the civil rights movement in person, not from a desk in New York. Reed had likely been sent to Gamecock City because, having been raised in Piney, Arkansas, he was an admitted "hick-talking Arkansawyer," and that went a long way in Gamecock City when talking to white folks.

The other reporter sent to Gamecock City, Paul Delaney, was black. Delaney was a short, somewhat stocky man who wore square eyeglass frames and sported a close-cut hairstyle. Born in Montgomery, Alabama, Delaney was a trailblazer. He sold copies of the *Alabama Journal* on the streets of Montgomery and became an army radio operator. Eventually promoted to be the *Times'* Deputy National Editor in 1980, he also helped found the Association of Black Journalists. Delaney became the *Times'* first black editor.

Strategically speaking, the *New York Times* covered its bases well by sending these two Southerners for a couple of weeks to Gamecock City. The reporting was fair, if not always accurate. (Delaney's favorite quotation was "Be cool.") Neither tried to do a hatchet job on the riven city's real-time grapple with total desegregation. After all, add a little misinformation to the mix and the whole city could've exploded into bloodshed.

By this time, the South was leading the nation in desegregation of schools. According to the United States Government, 38 percent of all black students in the American South were attending integrated schools in the Class of 1971's senior year.

However, the Northern states and the Western states were stuck at a static 27 percent during this same time period.

Reed and Delaney interviewed the Cub Man, who, reacting to the former Lincoln High student's disenchantment with their new school, said, "It makes you back off and shut the door." Ned Parker went further, saying, "The [b]lacks don't seem to have as much self-discipline. [They're] a little untamed. [T]hey probably had inferior teachers."

Whoa. Putting aside that last remark (which would not have been well-received in the faculty lounge), these two gentlemen from the *Times* described the big picture, the sky-high view, that blacks and whites – too caught up in our petty battles – were unable to see objectively.

The *Times* reported some obvious things. Blacks and whites sat at different tables in cafeterias and in classes. Few whites showed up for the three school dances.

The reporters also found that things were not always as they appeared on the surface. Wilbert Earl Robin of the Black Heritage Club (described by the *New York Times* as one of the more "militant blacks" but who had a white female friend) put it well when he said, "We all go to the same school, but everybody's got his own thing going."

The "*Us v. Them*" cliques in the Class of '71 were not necessarily comprised of former Lincoln High students versus white students. Sometimes, black students like the Ferguson twins, who'd attended white schools before total desegregation had begun, knew more former Edmunds students than those black students formerly at Lincoln High.

Vera Chisholm, Co-Editor of the newspaper, *The Cock's Quill*, had her opinions on the subject. She thought the black students who'd previously come over during the freedom-of-choice years were, well, a little snobbish and that they identified more with white students. Of course, she was 17 years old at the time talking to a *New York Times* reporter when she supposedly voiced these opinions. She might've mellowed a bit with age, or the reporting could have been inaccurate.

• • •

Who were the real heroes and heroines? That's easy. It was those few, vastly outnumbered blacks who'd come to white schools *before* total desegregation took place in 1970. They're the ones who had to field racial slurs, who were threatened and beaten up, and who probably feared each new school day. Some of that continued on both sides of the color line after total desegregation took place. However, there's a whole different dynamic between having one black student in a class as opposed to when half of the students in a classroom are black. Morris Workman described the experience well in a *New York Times* article:

My mother forced me to go to Alice Drive, [(a white junior high school,) and] I caught hell…Every time I turned around I was getting hit with a book. I was getting called "nigger" all the time, by teachers and students.

He was the only black kid in his class.

C.A. Wilson was another transfer from a black school to Alice Drive Junior High. On his first day of eighth grade, the teacher called the class roll. When it got to Clement A. Wilson's name, she called him "*Ce*ment" (as in concrete) Wilson. Great. Just what the new black guy wants on his first day in the white school.

It wasn't an accident that C.A. left his prior school and wound up at the white school. The Board needed to get some black faces into the white schools, but not just *any* black faces. As Dr. McArthur put it, the Board began to specifically recruit "bright and non-confron*ta*tional black students." Put another way, they were recruiting students who would follow the Golden Rule and turn the other cheek. C.A. was no pushover, but he was a nice guy.

We heard about C.A. soon after football season started in the 8th Grade. He played for Alice Drive Junior High School, which was our rival school at McLaurin Junior High School. It was the same as Carolina v. Clemson and Alabama v. Auburn, but on a way smaller scale. The talk was that Alice Drive had this running back named C.A. Wilson who could not be stopped. Simply could not. Every year we played Alice Drive it was a track meet. C.A. ran up and down the field scoring touchdowns.

C.A. had a way of spinning when he got hit that made tacklers lose their grip. It was a joy to watch, but despite his abilities, C.A. was not physically big. Heck, he was thin as a reed. But after a few spectacular football seasons in junior high and high school, the same guys at Alice Drive who'd been calling him dirty words started to treat him like a buddy. It must've been tough for him. I wouldn't have transferred to the predominately white schools had I been C.A. Wilson. I'm far too much of a chicken. Not in a million years, bud.

Another test case for the school board and the federal courts was Lynn, a young girl in town. Her daddy was a new lawyer, just setting up a practice downtown in Gamecock City. However, he had recently won a landmark case against Gamecock City's District 17, so Ernest Finney, Jr. was winning no popularity contests amongst the white folks in town. Still, he and his wife called Superintendent McArthur one weekend and asked for a tour of Central Elementary School. She'd be the only black girl in that school. The teachers were fair, but as you might expect, she was taunted by white kids. She eventually finished Central Elementary School, then went on to graduate from Gamecock City High School, and ultimately became a college professor. Her brother, Chip, is now the prosecutor in the judicial circuit where Gamecock City is located.

These were only a few of the black students who came over to the white schools. All of them faced the same fears and anxieties. All of them are brave folks in my book.

Anyway, the *New York Times* reporters Delaney and Reed were from a school of journalism that's largely passed us by. It would've been easy for these reporters to just paint the white folks in Gamecock City as racists (as did Judge Waties Waring's wife at her speech at the YMCA), throw out a few sensational paragraphs, then head over to the Cassarena Lounge on 378 for some pinball and cans of Old Milwaukee.

Instead, they neither pulled punches nor demonized Gamecock Cityites on *either* side of the color line. I can't help but wonder if they would still report the Class of 1971's painful struggles today as they had done had back then.

CHAPTER FIFTEEN

The Aftermath

After the riots and other confusion, the school schedule at Gamecock City High School completely dissolved. We had to return to campus on October 28th to meet in our home rooms (in my case, the chorus room) to have "rap sessions." In the '60s and early '70s, a "rap session" was a small meeting held to discuss some pressing issue or solve a conflict. And so, we rapped. There was a spirit of compromise – no Huey Newton or white supremacy polemics – and it became clear that some of the black students were resentful of how militants had hijacked the peace process. Other students were resentful of the student council members. Supposedly, the student council had adopted a Pollyanna 'tude and was too quick to claim that everything at school was rosy. I suspect that each session had its own dynamic and opinions. This group therapy was serving its purpose, mainly as a catharsis.

As part of the District's plan, the rap sessions were to be followed by a meeting of all black students in the auditorium and all white students in the gymnasium. However, five minutes before the bell rang, some of the student leaders impressed upon the District the need to have all black and white students meet together. Get it out in the open and all, that sorta thing. This just shows you how freaked the District was. In light of the recent riot and increasing tension, the joint meeting between the warring parties could've been disastrous.

The bell rang, and the student body shuffled into the auditorium (now called Patriot Hall). Black students sat together up front, and whites sat in the back. On the stage were members of various education-related boards, some of whom were black and most of whom were white.

The officials on stage talked a little peace, love, and understanding, then turned the microphone over to the students. As reported in the *Daily Item* on October 29th, the complaints outweighed the compliments, which is pretty much what one would expect. A student questioned the need for cops coming to the school, arguing the case for turning control of the zoo over to the animals. Another speaker wanted to let the students solve the problems rather than the faculty (which supposedly was causing them). A student, who'd been ostracized because he'd tried to help calm things during the riot, defended himself.

Slowly, the meeting turned raucous, so the District turned to Plan C, namely that black students would continue to meet alone in the auditorium and that white students would walk to the gymnasium for their meeting. I have absolutely no recollection of the white students' meeting, which tells me that I blew off the rest of the day.

However, the *Daily Item* noted that they had their own issues at the white students' meeting. Some white students complained that girls were objects of threats in school restrooms, were shoved about in hallways, and were generally treated in an arrogant manner. Also, why, they wondered, was "Dixie" banned when the band was allowed to play soul music? (Well, for starters, you can dance to Wilson Pickett, but you can't dance to "Dixie.") As in the meeting with black students, some preached nonviolence and understanding. These students told it from the heart, with one female student breaking down in tears while speaking.

Some students voiced resentment against blacks disrespecting the playing of the national anthem. Apparently, black "militants" had been raising their fists in the black power salute while the national anthem was playing. On the other hand, in a letter to the editor, there was a charge by Co-Student Body President Larry Blanding of inaccurate reporting on the *Daily Item*'s part. He disagreed with *The Item*'s description of certain black students as "militants"; instead, he argued that they were merely "[c]oncerned black students."

Then, there was the Black Heritage Club (BHC). Frankly, the BHC had some valid points, but on other issues, they just seemed to just be reciting Stokely Carmichael-isms. To some black and white students, the club seemed to be encouraging a fractious spirit within the student body with its incantations of black power, tiresome demands about transfer of control to the students, and fulminations about inequality. White students had no organization similar to the Black Heritage Club. Of course, the white students didn't *need* one. The superintendent was white, the school board was controlled by an ironclad white majority (in fact, the Board was all white except for one black man, Jim Solomon), and the law enforcement agencies were mainly white.

● ● ●

In any event, this new way of returning to school was be*yond* excitement for the Class of '71. We didn't have to go to classes! We guys got to walk girls to their cars. As far as I was concerned, this was welcome relief from the tedium of scholarship.

It might have been around this time that the white students had their eureka moments. One black female student at the meeting in the auditorium made it clear: "We didn't *ask* to come to this school." The white students, in turn, realized that many of these former Lincoln High folks didn't *want* to attend our happy little predominantly white school. They didn't even seem to *like* us. On the other hand, many ex-Lincolnites wistfully looked back and saw their old school with its clubs, sports teams, and traditions gone forever.

To say that all ex-Lincolnites hated the new Gamecock City High School is surely a lie. Kids adapt quickly, and we were all just kids. Many, if not most, students from the old Lincoln High thrived at the new school after things calmed down.

I personally don't buy white guilt. However, as for the Class of '71's black students' resentment of white folks? Well, there were obvious reasons for it, even though the white seniors at Gamecock City High School hadn't caused the problem. True, Gamecock City was beginning to leave Jim Crow behind, but the white students really didn't know what it'd been like to grow up under that system.

Here's an example: for many years, a popular booklet was published in New York City and sold across the United States. It was called the *Negro Travelers' Green Book: For Vacation Without Aggravation,* or just the *Green Book* for short. White members of the Class of '71 didn't need the *Green Book,* and though I might be wrong, I suspect that precious few white students had even *heard* of it. Still being published, right into the Class of '71's senior year, the *Green Book* was solely for use by black folks. The reason for the booklet was so that when black Americans traveled around the United States, they'd know which restrooms, hotels, restaurants, and other businesses would allow them to enter and which would have a hotel manager or restaurant hostess shaking her head upon their arrival. The *Negro Travelers' Green Book* was in no way limited to the Southern states. In fact, it covered most states in the nation, from California to New York City and from Ohio to Texas.

The 1957 edition of the *Green Book* listed four businesses in Gamecock City: the Edmonia Shaw Tourist Home at 206 Manning Avenue; the Mrs. Julia E. Byrd Tourist Home at 504 North Main Street; the C.H. Bracey Tourist Home at 210 West Oakland Avenue; and the Johnnie Williams Tourist Home on Highway 15A. If travelers didn't have local friends or family in

Gamecock County and the tourist homes were booked, they'd better move on.

Imagine what a pain all *that* must've been. The *Green Book* eventually ceased publication when federal civil rights legislation made it unnecessary, but thoughts of such things surely colored some former Lincolnites' mindsets as they walked into Gamecock City High School.

• • •

Two young students at McLaurin Junior High and Gamecock City High were aware of the difficulty in traveling. On the same day my parents received the Report to Parents flyer announcing total desegregation of Gamecock City's schools, the parents of two rising juniors living across town also received a copy of the same flyer. Fernaundra and Yulaundra Ferguson were both pretty, diminutive twins who became Gamecock High cheerleaders and members of the ROTC Angel Flight. They each had short afro hairdos and ready smiles. Fernaundra said that she didn't like to cause dissension and was somewhat shy. However, it was my perception that neither she nor her twin necessarily ran from political confrontations, nor lacked a willingness to speak out against a perceived wrong. We never personally met in Gamecock City, but I always held them in awe.

The Ferguson twins were proud daughters of a United States Air Force Master Sergeant and his wife, both from Gamecock City. The family was politically involved, and at Gamecock City High School, that translated into membership in the Black Heritage Club.

In the past, when their dad had been transferred to a new air base, the Ferguson twins would pack up and drive there with him and their mom. This included traveling as far as California by car. Fernaundra remembers that their parents were very protective of their daughters. Trips were planned in advance so that the family would be near an airbase when night descended. That way their parents knew there'd be no trouble finding a place to lay their heads.

The family returned to Gamecock City right in the middle of the freedom-of-choice era when their dad was assigned to Southeast Asia during the Vietnam War. Too young for Selma or the marches on Washington, D.C., the twins' politics were largely confined to what they saw as inequalities in the desegregation of Gamecock City High.

However, having attended Gamecock High their sophomore year, the Fergusons were suspected by some incoming Lincolnite students as collaborating with the enemy (i.e., the white students). On the other hand, some white students didn't seem receptive to the twins coming to "their" school.

Nonetheless, it was a long way from their childhood when just going to a movie was a reminder that they were seen as second-class citizens.

• • •

Total school desegregation in 1970-71 gave rise to probably the longest continuous series of trials in the city's history. On January 5, 1971, rumors spread that something was in the wind. Part of the diaspora was homesick and missed Lincoln more than ever. Rumblings were spreading across the student body about a demonstration of civil disobedience. The school board of trustees got word of it all. And they had a plan. Sorta.

Just over 110 black students gathered in the gymnasium and refused to go to class. The school board's administrators leapt to action in what became a semi-comical policing presence by faculty designed to keep the peace. Any school staffer who could walk, except secretaries, was mobilized. The mighty host descended upon Gamecock City High School like a cloud of locusts. The administrators waited outside the gymnasium's doors with cameras and tape recorders that they'd previously stocked up on for just such an occasion to preserve all evidence that they could. The boycotting students, as you'd expect, got bored. They'd made their point. They had grown weary of staying cooped up in the gymnasium, so they walked out.

The posse of paparazzi administrators was ready in the gym foyer. They photographed everything, including a couple of students busting a few windows on the way to class. Real law enforcement was summoned, and that was the beginning of the end of that. Putting aside the bloodletting on Kurt Weatherly and a few others on both sides of the color line, some fistfights, and a few knife-pulls, it was harmless, mildly disruptive fun with political overtones. Not too shabby for the first real social interaction in history of descendants of slave owners and their former slaves.

But, oh my goodness, while some students were given a suspension, other suspects had to be *tried*. Dr. Gregory Vaughn estimated the number of students who boycotted to be around 200. My guess is that the board hadn't thought this thing through. For the better part of the remaining school year, the District began a series of mini-trials, sometimes lasting from 6:30 p.m. to 10:00 p.m. – and all of this after finishing the trustees' regular day jobs. Each student who properly requested a hearing was given an opportunity to put forth his or her case. Very few attorneys were involved, though an ACLU lawyer showed up for a while. According to Superintendent McArthur, the ACLU attorney was "shiftlessly lazy, unprepared, and certainly not effective. Where do they find such people?" Reading between the lines, I don't think he liked this guy....

• • •

If there was a historical counterpoint to South Carolina, it was Massachusetts. In the years leading up to the Civil War, Boston had been the heart of America's abolitionist movement. Conversely, South Carolina had been the land of slavery apologia. For all the sanctimony and finger pointing at South Carolina, Gamecock City got through the school year tolerably well compared to some other jurisdictions. Gamecock Cityites and most of South Carolina had already voluntarily desegregated its schools four years before Boston's debacle. Some might say that Boston was the Colonel Sanders of desegregation. Yeah, Bostonians knew how to do racism right.

If you ever wondered when metal detectors were first used in high schools, look to Massachusetts. Many Bostonians didn't take to desegregation, and in no way did they appreciate forced busing. Some would argue that the brunt of the attack on forced busing was borne by poor whites and poor blacks while affluent Bostonians in suburbia were spared.

W. Arthur Garrity Jr., the federal judge who was writing the rules, essentially created, or at least facilitated, a war zone. Surely, he didn't want the job. Nonetheless, he could've done it more fairly. Judge Garrity decided to adopt a plan already developed by the Massachusetts State Board of Education. It was a reasonable approach to take, except that implementation of the plan was a disaster. The judge used forced busing to mix Boston's most dysfunctional white school (here read: poor Irish kids) with its most dysfunctional black school (here read: poor black kids). The only things these two schools excelled at were street fighting and pitiful academic scores.

To sum up the Boston experience, there's a Pulitzer prize winning photograph entitled *The Soiling of Old Glory* taken in 1976 by Stanley Forman that says it all. Theodore Landsmark, a young Boston civil rights lawyer, had the bad luck of walking out of City Hall in Boston on April 5, 1976. Landsmark was wearing a conservative brown three-piece suit. In the midst of a raggedy crowd of white protesters, he was grabbed and held by a plump white boy while another boy took an American flag on a flagpole and used it to attack Landsmark. It evokes every sympathetic fiber in the human body.

In another singular moment in American history, black Bostonian teenagers threw rocks at a white man's car passing by. The man crashed his car. The teenagers dragged him from the vehicle and crushed his skull with paving stones. The cops finally showed up. The crowd of teenagers, allegedly about a hundred of them, had circled the white man who was now in a coma. They chanted, "Let him die! Let him die!"

A white boy was stabbed nearly to death in South Boston. In retaliation, white residents of the area mobbed the school and held the black kids as prisoners. Nothing like that happened as part of court-ordered desegregation in Gamecock City, or for that matter, the entire state of South Carolina.

CHAPTER SIXTEEN

The Class of '71 Vanishes into the Future

Wait a minute, now. What's *this* all about?

Last year, the Class of '70 had an exciting graduation ceremony. Black power fists and diplomas were alleged to have been aflame at graduation. Remember how our school superintendent, a decorated combat veteran, was shaken to his core by the protests? Surely the mighty Class of '71 isn't going out like a friggin' *lamb*? Well, yes, bubba. Yes, it is.

At our graduation on June 1st, the Class of '71 went placidly. No one set themselves afire, politically speaking. My classmates offered no real disruptions that I recall. Granted, "The Man" had revamped the graduation procedure to avoid political protests anyway. It was as if the members of the Class of '71 had poked their heads out of the hole on Groundhog Day, grabbed their

Suppose They Gave a War, and Nobody Came posters, and ducked back underground.

As for "The Kid," I was a bit frazzled on graduation day. I had given our maid, Janet, my graduation gown to use as a robe in her church choir. However, I *meant* for Janet to take it home *after* graduation day. The fact that she had already taken it home to Saint Charles, which was 20 miles away in the opposite direction of my graduation ceremonies, wasn't discovered until my father was driving me to the stadium for the ceremony to begin. He swung the car around and drove me to St. Charles to retrieve the gown at record-breaking (for him, anyway) speeds. I made it to the stadium as the Class of '71 was literally walking in a long, snaking line to its seats.

And so, the Class of '71 flew out of Memorial Stadium, our wings still wet from birth. Until the mundane tribulations of life came knocking, my classmates spent the summer bumping their heads on the stars. After the ceremony, Miss McKissick and I went to some parties, which were being held around town, most of which were separate gatherings of mainly black and mainly white classmates. We'd already retreated to our own tribes an hour after the corpse was dead. Habits are hard to break. Wimp that I was, I had Miss McKissick back at her parents' house well before midnight with no more than a peck at the front door. Like I said – I was no threat to girls.

Within 30 days, I was sitting in blue jeans on the University of South Carolina's Green Horseshoe with my roommate-to-be Rusty Moore, attending freshman orientation hosted by some God-awful, pompous sophomore. Cub Man was up at Clemson practicing with the freshman football team, and Nedro was driving his father's tractor in Eastover, about to matriculate at Davidson College.

And so, what happened to the rest of the Class of '71?

• • •

I got a call in 2006 from my old bandmate, Gantt Williams. He asked if I'd be up for a practice with The Tempests, our boyhood soul band. The Tempests wanted to revive almost 40 years after we'd disbanded in the 1960s. Nancy Howle Patterson, our class mother, was organizing a 40-year reunion to be called a "Gathering of Friends." Most of The Tempests were in the Class of '71, and in some ways, we were the class band.

I was a little hesitant at first. I hadn't played music in a while at that point. I dropped out of the University of South Carolina for ten years to play music before receiving my history and law degrees. But after getting my diplomas, music reentered my life in the late 1990s. I'd started occasionally playing music with a Mount Pleasant neo-soul group called the East Coast Party Band. The Party Band was packed with excellent musicians and singers. A fun bunch of people. Still, I wanted to be known as a lawyer, not a musician. Unlike some jobs, it really matters in the legal world that you're perceived as competent, reliable, and professional. These days, although I agree that lawyers must have good reputations and must not step out of the bounds of propriety, attorneys can (and should) do just about anything for fun that he or she wants (within reason) in their spare time and not hurt their reputation.

Unfortunately, I was a little behind on realizing this reality of the legal world when a defining moment happened at Alhambra Hall in Mount Pleasant, South Carolina. The East Coast Party Band was booked to play a wedding reception, and the regular keyboard player was indisposed. I agreed to do the job. Later, I learned that I'd have to wear a tux, which in itself was enough to make me want to cancel; however, I'd said I'd play, and I couldn't go back on my word. At the reception, I walked over to the food table and then headed downstairs. Coming upstairs at the same time was Charlie Goldberg of the Steinberg Law Firm. He was an invitee to the reception. Charlie and I had tried some jury trials together. He was a heck of a courtroom lawyer, and as a former President of the Charleston Bar Association, a man entitled to respect.

Charlie looked me up and down in my tux.

"You servin' drinks or waitin' tables?" Charlie asked.

That did it for another seven years until Gantt called.

• • •

Gantt told me that the reunion job apparently involved no tux-edo, and I quickly agreed. Our first get-togethers were at a mobile home park outside of Aiken. After a passable first rehearsal, we moved practices to the service bay of a car dealership in Gamecock City where we'd practiced as junior high school boys. Owned at the time by our drummer Jim Jones and his brother John, the auto dealerships seemed large enough to incorporate as a small town. Thus, we nicknamed it "Jonesville" and eventually recorded a music CD there entitled *Return to Jonesville*.

Having not seen most of The Tempests in more than three decades, I was apprehensive about how they'd act and look. Certainly, we'd all gone off in different directions as far as our careers were concerned. Guitarist Jimmy Brown lives in Chester, New Jersey and is an engineer for Google. Gantt, our singer and former drummer, graduated from Clemson University with an economics degree and worked as a comptroller for several busi-nesses right there in Gamecock City. Bryan Hatfield, vocals and trumpet, owns several insurance agencies.

Billy Brown, our bass player, lived in the Augusta area and worked at the Savannah River Nuclear Plant before retiring, but while we were practicing at the trailer park, Billy Boy lived at a nearby nudist camp in Aiken County. Kurt Weatherly, our other trumpeter and the boy who had been beaten up in the school gymnasium at Gamecock City High School, is a golf pro. Carl Sinkler, band director and an inductee into the South Carolina State University Jazz Hall of Fame, plays sax like Junior Walker.

Truthfully speaking, except for me of course, The Tempests pretty much look like a bunch of old geezers. However, we have a great time getting together. We sound pretty good for a band that plays once every four years. The best part of The Tempests experience is grilling cheeseburgers at Bryan's house on the Old Manning Road.

So, the big night of the Class of '71's reunion arrived.

We had set up our equipment at the Elks Club on Wedgefield Road. It's just a gunshot away from Gamecock City Speedway where the Klan held its ill-fated rally forty years earlier. The Tempests were wearing matching suits that would make the Famous Flames feel right at home. The Class of '71 lined up outside the door. Pretty soon, the place was packed. The Mighty Tempests were playing all the soul music hits, all the time. Not bad for a band whose last gig took place before Neil Armstrong set foot on the moon.

Playing in a band is like handling a boat at a dock. The hardest parts are getting your boat down the ramp, off the trailer, and into the water on one hand, then, on the other hand, getting the boat back up the ramp and onto the trailer again. Similarly, the biggest trouble for a band is starting the song at the same time, on the one hand, then ending the song together, on the other hand. We missed a few. But the liquor flowed, and as it did, the crowd seemed to like us better and better. Party on!

I got to talk to the Class of '71 on the breaks. It was quite difficult to recognize some of them, and I'm sure they had trouble figuring out who I was. We all had stickers with our names and class book pictures from *The Paragon*, the Class of '71's high school yearbook.

However, nobody had trouble recognizing Nedro Parker, our Senior Class President. Some folks just don't age like others, and Nedro still looked about the same. He'd quit Davidson College after a semester or two in the 1970s then moved to the Silverlake District of Los Angeles. Nedro spends his days in LA as a building contractor and an ersatz apologist and advocate for Scientology. He's become a crusader in Scientology's special ops war against drug companies, and he's appeared on television shows in Los Angeles. Parker and his Scientologist friends are anti-psychotropic-drug guerillas. Underfunded against the mega-billion-dollar pharmaceutical manufacturers, it's hard to see how they'll ever win *that* battle. But anybody who wants to take on the big pharmaceutical manufacturers has got to be doing something right, aye?

• • •

Cub Man, President of the Student Body, was there, too. Cub always wanted to play drums with The Tempests. But, because he still refused to keep the beat and instead rolled on the snare and tom-toms most of the time, we usually don't let him play. However, I think we were going to let him play *this* time, it being the reunion and all, but he skipped out early.

Upon graduation from high school, Cub played football at Clemson for a while then eventually graduated with an eye toward going into some line of business. His first project was Chanello's Pizza on Rosewood Drive in Columbia. It was directly across from the Taurus Club where my rock 'n roll band played, so I could walk across the street for pizza after we played. Cub bought framed photographs of famous stars for the restaurant's walls. Little vignettes were written on the photos saying things such as, "Cub, thanks for the best pizza in the world. Call me when you get to Memphis. Your buddy, Elvis."

As it turned out, Cub had a genius for sales, and I ain't talkin' pizza either. I'd known him since the first grade. I never guessed that his natural ability as a raconteur and fast talker was actually what people came to call a "marketable skill." He saw merit in a new field called telecommunications. I tried to tell him that telephones would always need to be connected to a wall by cords. I also emphasized to Cub that long-distance calls were expensive and that no one could afford to make them.

One day, years later, I took Cub on the intracoastal waterway in my Chris Craft cabin cruiser. It was then that I learned the Cub was rich. Real rich. What my daddy called, "I *mean* rich." Before he became wealthy, Cub Man offered me a job in his fledgling telecommunications company. I was no fool and, of course, refused.

"It's goh be *big*, Moeez," he claimed. "They comin' out with this thing called a *cell* phone. We go get *rich*, Moeez."

"Oh *no*, Cub, that ay gonna amount to nothin'," I said. "I ain't sellin' no telephones. No, I'm gonna be a trial *law*-yuh."

It's this incredible foresight and business acumen on my part that chains me to a conference room table at the office on Easter Sundays eating chicken strips while getting ready for trial on Monday mornings. Cub spends these type mornings counting his 22 million dollars, eating turkey with his children, and playing basketball at the gymnasium inside the Cubbage family compound in Fountain Inn, South Carolina. Hey, even the *janitor* at Cub's telecommunications business probably retired as a millionaire. Oh well. You gotta have a sense of humor.

● ● ●

I looked for Essex Durant, the Sex Machine, and his bud, Leon Pack at the Class of '71's reunion party. Essex eventually had stopped showing up for our Christmas campouts. I was off doing other things and hadn't heard from him in years. The Elks Club meeting room was jammed with my classmates and their spouses, but nobody looks quite like Essex Durant. I couldn't find him. Maybe we could get him on stage to do the funky chicken. Unfortunately, no news was bad news.

The Sex Machine was dead.

Essex loved to fish. It was his undoing. He'd been fishing with a friend in a little 14-foot jon boat. Essex wasn't wearing a life jacket. A storm crept onto Lake Marion and caught them by surprise. It was July 24, 2004, and they were only a few hundred yards away from Pack's Landing near Rimini, in Gamecock County. It took two days for divers to find his body. Essex was just in his early 30s.

I also learned that Leon Pack was dead, and his passing was even more tragic. It was what police call a domestic situation. As every cop knows, domestic conflicts are often the most dangerous of all. Leon's girlfriend was leaving him. Leon holed himself into a room and got into a shootout with the police. They said he'd reloaded his weapon three times in the standoff. Finally, Leon shouted out that he was surrendering. The door lock clicked. It seemed as if things were going to be OK. Then, Leon shot himself. That's what the police said. May Leon rest in peace.

The Class of '71 had lost several more classmates by the time of the reunion. Looking at their unwrinkled faces in *The Paragon*, it's hard to believe they're gone. "Fabulous Freddie" Solomon was there. He was fighting a losing battle with colon cancer at the time. Freddie retired after 11 years in the NFL. He retired to Florida where he continued to mentor young men and set up a scholarship fund until he died.

May they rest in peace. But the reunion was far from unhappiness.

Some of the ladies at the reunion saw opportunities to return a slight, still smoldering after all the years. Analiese had her chance to even the score with Ella, who'd stolen her beau in high school. Ella and the beau married. However, after 30 years of marital bliss, the husband took a girlfriend and eventually ran off with the wench. Ella was destroyed by the whole thing. Analiese's blow was struck in the Elks Club's ladies' room. The two women were applying eyeliner and lipstick at side-by-side mirrors. I wasn't there, of course, but this is what I'm *told* happened.

"Well, *hey*, Ella," Analiese said. "Long time no see."

"Sometimes it's better not to see," Ella replied with a sniff.

Analiese was tight, having had several multicolored drinks. By now, Analiese thought that everything she said was hilarious. Also, like me, she'd not gotten into J. Grady Locklear's English class which might've given her the tools to express herself more eloquently.

Now, there were two elephants in the room. One was this business about Ella's husband dumping her for the girlfriend after all those years of marriage. The other elephant, you might say, was Ella herself. Ella had put on some weight. A *lot* of weight. About 100 pounds worth, roughly speaking.

It would've been rude to mention it, but Analiese would not be denied. She killed two elephants with one stone:

"Honey," said Analiese. "What's the difference between a wife and a girlfriend?"

"I don't know," Ella said. "What?"

"About 100 pounds," Analiese answered, laughed out loud, and winked at Ella. "It's Slow Gin *Fizz*ie Time!" she said, walking out the door.

C.A. Wilson, and Joye, his bride of many years, were there too. As everyone expected, C.A. had done well for himself. The year after the Class of '71 graduated, C.A. started in the defensive backfield for Paul Dietzel at the University of South Carolina. If Dietzel had better sense, he would've played C.A. more at running back, and the University of South Carolina might've done better than 42-53-1 during his tenure there. C.A. graduated with a five-year pharmacy degree and came back to live in Gamecock City.

Thomas Sumpter, who'd been through the Class of '71's voluntary desegregation years at McLaurin Junior High School, made an appearance. Thomas retired from the United States Army as a colonel and has prospered after retirement in the business world. He was his usual somewhat quiet, but always friendly, self. It also was good to see Moses Geddis, an early freedom-of-choice transfer who, like a few other brave souls, had transferred into the white schools and became part of them.

The Ferguson twins didn't attend the school reunion, though. Odd because both have enjoyed successful careers in academics. Fernaundra Ferguson first graduated from Bennett College in Greensboro, North Carolina, then from Howard University, School of Law in Washington, D.C.

Eventually she married, had a son, practiced law, and secured a teaching position at the University of West Florida. There, Fernaundra retired as an assistant dean.

She now works at the Lampkin Law Firm in Gamecock City and is a board member of the Association for Conflict Resolution (ACR), an alternative-dispute-resolution group.

Fernaundra emphasizes that though she works in a law office, she doesn't practice law.

"High school was not that bad," Fernaundra said to me when we spoke last. "It was not that bad." She and her sister had been an integral part of the Class of '71, attended the school prom, and had some good times. However, the desegregation itself was chaotic and brought its own set of worrisome memories.

Her twin, Yulaundra Ferguson-Heyward, also graduated from Bennett College in Greensboro, married and had children, and did well, enjoying a successful career as the Assistant Director of the Counseling and Testing Center at Francis Marion University in nearby Florence.

Chief Justice Ernest Finney's daughter Nikky Finney didn't attend the reunion, to my knowledge anyway. However, she's since gone on to win the Wallace Stevens Award, a one in a lifetime honor presented by the Academy of American Poets.

But one blemish on the face of the Class of '71 will never heal, and thank God he didn't appear at the reunion. Donald "Pee Wee" Gaskins had died on September 6, 1991. His last murder, among his many other killings, was of another Death Row inmate, Rudolph Tyner. He blew Tyner's head off with high explosives. Pee Wee said in his book *Final Truth* that, "[M]y lawyer, Jack Swerling, tried to defend me the best he could, but it was obviouser (sic) than hell that the Court and everyone else was determined to *get Pee Wee Gaskins*." Pee Wee walked into that execution room with no help and a smile on his face. So anyway, Gaskins was not on the dance floor shaggin' to The Tempests at the reunion. Long may he burn.

As the Temptations said, "And the band played on." It all went well. A substantial number of the Class of '71 looked better than they had in high school. I was happy to see that the crowd was not all white or not all black and hoped that at the next reunion, we'd have more of the former Lincoln group. After all, we're too old to fight, and even if we did, nobody would get hurt.

Epilogue

The Return to Gamecock City

So, what about the rest of these Gamecock City characters? My immediate family has vanished from Gamecock City, though I do have a vivacious grandson, Brayden Locklear, and many wonderful cousins on the Harritt side there. My dad and mother are dead and in heaven.

Sister Elizabeth Scott Moise became the ultimate "Comeback Kid." You might say she's like Thanksgiving dinner – better the next day after it's been reheated. Although Scott wasn't accepted into law school the first time she applied, she was admitted the next year and tore the place apart. By the time she graduated, Scott was unanimously elected Editor-in-Chief of the *South Carolina Law Review* and won the Claude Sapp Award for the law student most likely to succeed. Years later, the University of

South Carolina Law School presented her with the Compleat Lawyer Award. Now she teaches at the same University of South Carolina Law School that wouldn't let her in at first.

Baby Sister Roo, the little girl once afraid of the "man in the attic" at bedtime, was a dietician at the Dorn VA Hospital in Columbia until this past fall. Knowing her bullheadedness, um, I mean ten*ac*ity, she probably was running the place by the time she retired. I'll bet the VA Hospital Director still calls her each morning to get his daily marching orders. She's the only one of us five brothers and sisters who went straight through college without dropping out. More incredibly, I think Claire can do math.

Big Brother Ben is a legend in Charleston and an author. He gets a lot of press, being written up in gourmet and hunting magazines every few months. My official name in the Holy City is "Ben Moise's Brother." And by the way, he did finally pass Statistics and got a master's degree after that.

Brother Mike lives in Loris and plays golf pretty regularly. He no longer teaches history or coaches football for Gamecock City High or the Fighting Lions of Loris High School. Like our big brother, Coach Moise is a legend unto himself in Loris. Being near the coast, Loris High School abounds with shrimp-baiters and fishermen. It was rumored that when one of his senior students was on the borderline between an F and a D and might not graduate, Coach Moise let him know that his final decision about the grade might be enhanced by a pound of creek shrimp or some fresh tuna. (Who would dispute that bringing fresh shrimp to class constitutes above-average class participation?) Just as Brother Ben paid for my first lawyer outfit at Max's Men's Shop in Charleston, Mike paid my automobile liability insurance while I was in undergraduate school.

These days, I travel to the Gamecock City to see Brayden play t-ball and play in Memorial Park. A while back, my daughter and I just drove around town looking at how it's changing, and reciting family and Gamecock City history. Since I've gotten older, I've had many questions about Gamecock City and my family, and I've wanted to go ask Mom or Dad about them.

Now they're gone. I can't recall what enlightenment I've given my daughter on family matters, so I tell her the same things over and over. She must love that.

As for the city itself, Gamecock City has good bones. It's bouncing back. Population is growing. There's a Hyatt Hotel downtown and several upscale restaurants. Volunteer opportunities are everywhere, which have always been sort of a signature of the City.

Some things never change, though.

My childhood home at 230 Church Street in Gamecock City still stands. It's owned by a medical doctor with big dogs and is nicely renovated. I told my daughter that the basement has Cub's and my names still painted on the brick wall from the days when it was our clubhouse. Ho hum.

• • •

My daughter and I drove down Church Street toward Main Street and past Temple Sinai. Temple Sinai is the only game in Gamecock County, if you're a Jew. My great-great-grandfather's name is still inscribed on one of the stained-glass windows. Temple Sinai is in immaculate condition, well-painted, and perfectly landscaped, but the thriving, almost frenetic Jewish community that helped build Gamecock City is dying. Literally.

The average age at the Temple is roughly 80-years-old. When these folks are gone, the shofar will blow no more, and Temple Sinai will forever close its doors as a living active congregation. Abe Stern, who's attended the temple for half a century, admits that there's nothing much in Gamecock City for single young folks to do. As a child, Gamecock City was rife with young Jews my age. Pretty Jewesses were voted local beauty queens, and Jewish boys played football and other school sports. Half the town shopped at Berger's Department Store, the Capitol Department Store, Brody's Department Store, or Jack's.

But Temple Sinai doesn't have a full-time rabbi anymore. For many years, Rabbi Robert Seigel drove from Charleston to Gamecock City. Sixteen weeks each year, plus the high holidays, Rabbi Seigel presided. I lamented to him Temple Sinai's impending demise, but he accepted the reality of the thing. When I asked Rabbi Seigel why an entire generation abandoned Gamecock City, he attributed the decline to young Jews moving away to urban centers like Charleston or Columbia.

"Where do you live?" he asked.

"In Charleston," I said.

"There you have it," he replied.

Some Gamecock City Jews got along so well with the Protestants and Catholics that they married them. On June 2, 2018, the Temple Sinai Jewish History Center in affiliation with the Gamecock County Museum, opened to the public.

While in high school, my daughter mentioned that she had a book report to do on the Holocaust. We drove down the Old Manning Road, and I mentioned Abe Stern. "There's no better person to tell you about the Holocaust than Mr. Stern," I said. So, I called Abe and hinted about us driving over to chat with him. He wasn't feeling up to going over the Holocaust just then, and Lord knows we respected his wishes. Abe said he didn't want people to think that he was a whiner or playing the victim. Then he backtracked and said that he didn't think the Holocaust should be forgotten. He'd heard about the Klan claiming that no such thing took place.

"Come on down to the [Sunset Country] Club next time you're here, and we'll talk about it," Abe said.

In supreme irony, Former South Carolina Governor, Nikki R. Haley, and the Gamecock City Council proudly announced in 2011 that a company known as Continental Tire was building an immense manufacturing plant in Gamecock County on the Old Manning Road. Now its lights burn overhead in the night, setting the darkness free. According to at least one source:

"The German war machine needed lots of rubber and, as supplies of natural rubber became more difficult to get to Europe, synthetic rubber became the order of the day. Like many industrial opera-

tions in Germany at the time, Continental used Jewish slave labor supplied by the Nazis."

I feel sure that Continental denies any fault in the matter. Unlike Gamecock City's Temple Sinai, Continental, the company with roots in Germany, in whose asphalt tunnels Abe Stern toiled at the Ahlem slave labor camp, thrives after expanding into the United States when World War II ended. You might have some Continentals on your car.

• • •

Finally, at the end of our long drive, my daughter and I returned to Gamecock City. After a quick peck on the cheek from her, I began my two-hour drive back to Charleston. My mind rambled on about many things during that long drive. Mainly though, I thought how my world changed so much in what still seemed to be such a short time. I never suspected that I'd return as a divorced man or even that I'd ever file for a divorce. But life has a way of regenerating itself in time. All pain heals for those who want it to heal.

I'll never again be that five-year-old Southern boy in a coonskin cap playing in my neighborhood with Cubman, Nedro, and Cousin Billy, secure in the knowledge that my father and mother are nearby if trouble arises, and ignorant of the fact that every day they're busy battling life unto the death themselves.

The days of juking at the Po Boy Club in Timmonsville with Jeffrey Ray Sanford and our dates are just memories. After all, we both recently celebrated our one-year cardiac surgeries.

My face shows more age every time I look in the mirror, but that's God's gift. He ages us slowly, day-by-day, so we can adapt to it.

And once again, I'm relearning that every day is a priceless gift filled with hope. It's going to be alright for the Class of '71. Did we measure up to the task of being test cases for total school desegregation, the massive realignment that the white and black establishments thrust upon us as kids?

Should the brunt of total desegregation have been done in a different party of society other than public schools? Did it fulfill the dreams of Waties Waring and Thurgood Marshall?

Questions, questions. Hard to tell. But I'd like to believe that when confronted with a dangerous, and possibly deadly, coming together of two disparate worlds, together we took a small step on the road to reconciliation and peace. It wasn't bloody Mississippi, and it wasn't bloody Boston. Despite having been told what to do by our parents, our school administrators, the Citizens' Councils, the Ku Klux Klan, et alia, the Class of '71 did things its own way. By and large, the waters were still when we left those schools. And that's not too bad. No, brothers and sisters, it ain't bad at all.

About the Author

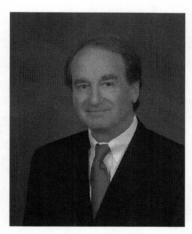

Warren Moise grew up in Sumter, South Carolina (a.k.a Gamecock City). He graduated high school with the Class of '71, the first totally desegregated class in the city's history. Later, Warren received degrees in History and Law from the University of South Carolina. He is a trial lawyer, author, and former adjunct professor at both of South Carolina's law schools. He has been invited to speak by the South Carolina Supreme Court at two South Carolina Judicial Conferences, and written numerous books published by the South Carolina Bar, articles published by the American Bar Association, and a legal column for the South Carolina Bar for 15 years. Warren has spoken at approximately

45 legal seminars over the years and has won various awards including the South Carolina Bar Trial and Appellate Advocacy Award, South Carolina Super Lawyers, Best Lawyers in America, Founding Fellow for the Litigation Counsel of America, and the Compleat Lawyer Gold Award from USC Law School. He has spent years researching the desegregation of Southern schools and the cultures of those students involved in desegregation, which ultimately resulted in this book.

Other Books by the Author

"So You're Going to Try Your First Case," SC Bar Publisher (5th ed. 2018).

"Beyond The Bar," SC Bar Publisher (2014).

"Premises Liability," in South Carolina Damages, SC Bar Publisher (2004).

"Credibility and Character Evidence: History, Policy and Procedure," 2 Volumes, SC Bar Ass'n Publisher (2001 & 2003).

Co-Editor with SC Court of Appeals Judge William L. Howard and Co-Author: "The South Carolina Practice Manual," 3 volumes, SC Bar Ass'n Publisher (2000-2003),

"Rebellion in the Temple of Justice," 1 Volume, iUniverse Publishers (2003).

"Impeachment Evidence: Attacking & Supporting the Credibility of Witnesses," S.C. Bar Ass'n Publisher (1996).

Sources Consulted

NOTES: The historical archives of *The Item*, [known variously as *The Item*, *The Gamecock City Item*, and *The Sumter Daily Item*,] have been used *passim*, in addition to the pinpoint citations given below. The same applies to Laurin Currie McArthur, Jr.'s book *The Pleasure of Remembering What Schools Can Do in South Carolina* (Furman U. 1997). Additionally, the citation forms are a combination of those used for legal citations, as well as standard English citation forms.

- Theodore Adams, *Somebody Had to Do It: First Children in School Desegregation* (Interview by Kenneth Cooper) (April 8, 2009) (desegregation of Orangeburg schools).

- Donald P. Baker, *Education's Cast-Offs: How Whites Avoid Integration and Leave*

- *Blacks Adrift* (1996).

- Jack Bass, *10 Members of Splinter Klan Charged With Rally Slaying* at A5 (Special to The Washington Post) (Sept. 17, 1970).

- Robert D. Bass, *Gamecock passim* (Sandlapper Pub. Co., Inc. 1961).

- Abram Louis Blanding, *James Dickey Blanding* <u>in</u> *Blanding-McFaddin: 1553-1906* at 23 (1927).

- *See* 2 Allan D. Thigpen, *The Illustrated Recollections of Potter's Raid April 5-21, 1865* at 321 (2d ed. 1998).

- VI Blanding Family, *The Book of Remembrance: Historical Facts of the Blanding Family 1846-1941* (1941).

- Larry Blanding, *Letter to the Editor: Resents Coverage, The Item* (Nov. 1970).

- James Brown, *Hot Pants*

- William Lewis Burke, *Matthew J. Perry: The Man, His Times, and His Legacy* (Burke and Gergel eds. 2004).

- Neil R. McMillen, *The Citizens' Council* at p. 182 (Univ. Of Illinois Press 1971) (map of South Carolina counties, including Gamecock County, with organized Councils).

- Charise Cheney, *Blacks on Brown: Intra-Community Debates Over School Desegregation in Topeka, Kansas, 1941-1955*, Western Historical Q. (Winter 2011 Oxford University Press).

- Mary Chesnut, *The Private Mary Chesnut* at 42 (emphasis in original).

- Chicago Tribune, *Holocaust claims: A number of major German companies face* (May 11, 1999).

- *Hemmings Sports & Exotic Car Magazine* (Oct. 2012); https://www.hemmings.com/magazine/hsx/2012/10/

Continental/3717091.html (background on Continental manufacturing role during WW II).

- Walter Edgar, *South Carolina: A History* (1998).

- Michael Fellman, *Citizen Sherman* at 264 & 453 n.5 (1995).

- Judge Richard Fields, Interview, May 3, 2019.

- William R. Fennell, III, *Joel Poinsett* in *Reflections III* at 133 (Sumter Fortnightly Club Papers 2003).

- Pee Wee Gaskins and Wilton Earle, *Final Truth: The Autobiography of a Serial Killer* (2004) *passim*. (Many of the quotations and much of the background information about Gaskins came largely from this book.)

- Anne King Gregorie, *History of Sumter County* (1954).

- Emma Harvin, *Somebody Had to Do It: First Children in School Desegregation* (Interview by Millicent Brown) (October 15, 2009) (desegregation of Sumter schools).

- Guardian, *The unspeakable truth about slavery in Mauritania* (2019).

- Tom Hanchett, *Saving the South's Rosenwald Schools* (2004).

- James Haw, *John and Edward Rutledge of South Carolina* (1997).

- *A History of the First Presbyterian Church, Sumter, South Carolina* 3 (1973).

- S. Pony Hill, *Strangers in Their Own Land: South Carolina's State Indian Tribes* (2009).

- William C. Hine, *South Carolina State University: A Black Land-Grant College in Jim Crow America* (U. S.C. Press 2018) (discussing role played by Fred Henderson Moore).

- Mary S. Hoffschwelle, *The Rosenwald Schools of the American South* (2006).

- Benjamin F . Hornsby, Jr., *Stepping Stone to the Supreme Court: Clarendon County, South Carolina* (S.C. Dept. Archives and History 1992).

- *The Item* (August 27, 1970) (Seneca school burns).

- *The Item* (August 27, 1970)) (rumors were problematic).

- Michael P. Johnson & James L. Roark, *Black Masters* (1984).

- Michael P. Johnson & James L. Roark, *No Chariot Let Down* (1984).

- Ira Kaye, *The Alice in Sumterland* in New South (June 1963).

- Zachary J. Lechner, *The South of the Mind: American Imaginings of White Southernness, 19601980* (September 15, 2018).

- Harriette Kershaw Leiding, *Historic Houses of South Carolina* (1921).

- Van King & Hubert Osteen, Jr., *Joint Meeting Fails: Trouble Deep - Rooted, The Item (*Oct. 29, 1970).

- Joseph Knight, *David Garrick* (1894).

- James G. Leyburn, *The Scotch-Irish: A Social History* (1962).

- J. Grady Locklear, various in-person conferences (2019).

- Rebecca Marlin and Sarah Mathewson, *Enforcing Mauritania's Anti-Slavery Legislation: The Continued Failure of the Justice System to Prevent, Protect and Punish*, Report (2015).

- Laurin Currie McArthur, Jr., *The Pleasure of Remembering What Schools Can Do in South Carolina* (Furman U. 1997).

- Karen F. McCarthy, *The Other Irish* (2011 Sterling Pub. Co.) (Scots-Irish migrations to America).

- David McCullough, *1776: The Illustrated Edition* (2007).

- W.A. McElveen, Jr., *A History of Sumter: Recalled With Post Cards* (Sumter Printing Co., Inc. 1995).

- W.A. McElveen, Jr., *Pocalla* in *Reflections III* at 244 (Sumter Fortnightly Club Papers 2005).

- III *Captain Francis Marion Moise, Jr., Sumter, SC, From the Family Files of the Queen: Pauline McFaddin Moise Harritt* (Catherine Vernon Moise ed. 2007).

- Benson J. Lossing, *History of the United States for Families and Libraries* (1857).

- Alva M. Lumpkin, *The Life and Times of Thomas Waties* (1994).

- Edward A. Miller, Jr., *Gullah Statesman: Robert Smalls from Slavery to Congress 1839-1915* (1995).

- Jessica McCulley, *Black Resistance to School Desegregation in St. Louis During the* Brown *Era* (Fall 2009). This appears to be an undergraduate history paper.

- William McIntosh, III, *Indians' Revenge: Including a History of the Yemassee Indian War* (2009).

- Tommy Mims, Telephone Interview Regarding Pee Wee Gaskins (Dec. 3, 2010.

- Miss Penina Moise, *Fancy's Sketch Book* (J.S. Burges Pub., Charleston S.C. 1833).

- Wesley Moore, *Tolerating Upper Middle Class Northern Transplants for Dummies* in *You Do Hoodoo?* (blog posting).

- Alfonso A. Narvaez, Clement Haynsworth Dies at 77, *Lost Struggle for High Court Seat* (N.Y. Times Nov. 23, 1989).

- Sue New, *The ATurks@ of Sumter County, South Carolina* (2005) (www.sciway3.net).

- Cassie Nicholes, *Historical Sketches of Sumter County* 433-34 (R.L. Bryan Co., Columbia S.C. 1975). *See also Hood v. Board of Trustees of Sumter County School District No. 2*, 295 F.2d 390 (4th Cir. 1961) (discrimination against Turks enjoined by the court *per curiam*).

- I-II John Belton O'Neall, *Biographical Sketches of the Bench and Bar of South Carolina* (1859).

- Vicenzo & Luigi Pappalettera, *The Brutes Have the Floor* (1970).

- Doug Pardue, *A Story of Two School Districts*, Charleston Post and Courier (Feb. 17, 2013).

- *Remembering the Fourth Circuit Judges: A History from 1941 to 1998*, 55 Wash. & Lee L. Rev. 471, 497 (1998) (bio of Clement F. Haynsworth, Jr.).

- Gerald M. Sider, *Lumbee Indian Histories: Race, Ethnicity, and Indian Identity in the Southeastern United States* (1993).

- W.T. Sherman to U.S. Grant, December 28, 1866, Correspondence in *Wild Life on the Plains and Horrors of Indian Warfare* at 120 (1891).

- *Abraham Stern Interview* (by Robert Buxton, Jewish Heritage Collection, College of Charleston 1999).

- *Abraham Stern*, Tel. Conversation (with the author 2011).

- Jeffrey Toobin, *Inside the Secret World of the Supreme Court* 6 (Anchor Books 2007) (Chief Justice Rehnquist working in Stanford Law cafeteria).

- Thomas S. Sumter, *Stateburg and Its People* (2d ed. 1949).

- Sumter County Soil and Water Conservation District, *An Affiliate Tour of Marston Plantation, Edgehill Plantation, and the Ruins of Sans Souci in Historic Stateburg, South Carolina* (2009).

- I-II *The Illustrated Recollections of Potter's Raid April 5-21, 1865* (Thigpen ed. 2007).

- The New York Times, *Klan Leader and 9 Accused in Carolina Of a Robbery Plot* (Sept. 18, 1970) (Robert E. Scoggin, Grand Dragon, KKK).

- Robert J. Thomas, *Confessions of a Federal Judge's Law Clerk* (2011) (District Judge Timmerman's clerk).

- Thomas Tisdale, *A Lady of the High Hills: Natalie DeLage Sumter* (2001).

- Time Magazine, *Nation: Judge Clement Haynsworth* (Aug. 29, 1969).

- Stephen Tompkins, *John Wesley: A Biography* (Eerdmans Pub. 2003).

- United Daughters of the Confederacy, South Carolina Chapter, *Recollections and Reminiscences: 1861–1865 Through World War I* (S.C. Chapter, U.D.C. 1990).

- United States Department of State,

- United States Holocaust Memorial Museum, *Holocaust Encyclopedia: The 84th Infantry Division*, www.ushmm.org/wic/en/article.php? Accessed on Nov. 24, 2011.

- Gregory L. Vaughn, *With All Deliberate Resistance* (1987).

- I-III David Duncan Wallace, *The History of South Carolina passim* (1934).

- Essie Mae Washington-Williams & William Stadiem (contributor), *Dear Senator: A Memoir by the Daughter of Strom Thurmond* (2005).

- Sammy Way, *Nathalie deLage Sumter* (*Sumter Item*, posted October 16, 2016).

- Robert Wernick et al., *Blitzkrieg* 18 (Time-Life Books Inc. 1977) (German attack on Poland).

- Juan Williams, *Thurgood Marshall: American Revolutionary* (*Times Books* 1998).

- *2 The Carolina Backcountry on the Eve of the Revolution, 1766, 1767, 1768* (Richard J. Hooker ed., U.N.C. Press 1953) (references to Rev. Charles Woodmason).

- Works Progress Administration, *A History of South Carolina* (1941).

Case law

Green v. County School Board of New Kent County, 391 U.S. 430 (1968) (freedom of choice system generally ineffective).

Griffin v. County School Board, 377 U.S. 218, 234 (1964) (time for all deliberate speed has run).

Brown v. Board of Education, 347 U.S. 483 (1954).

Hood v. Board of Trustees of Sumter County School District No. 2, 295 F.2d 390 (4th Cir. 1961) (discrimination against Turks enjoined by the court *per curiam*).

Randall v. Board of Trustees of Sumter County, 232 F. Supp. 786 (E.D.S.C. 1964) (*Randall #1*) (barring continuing segregation).

Randall v. Board of Trustees of Sumter County, 241 F. Supp. 787 (E.D.S.C. 1965) (*Randall #2*) (freedom of choice).